MW00747935

Sharing our Journeys
(Queer Elders Tell Their Stories)

Ku Sud

Edited by Ron Kearse

Filidh Publishing

Filidh Publishing, Victoria, BC.

ISBN 978-1-927848-38-8 (Soft Cover)

Cover Design by Danny Weeds
Cover photo title: Gay March on Queen's Park Toronto 1976
Photo by: Charles Dobie
Artistic Treatments by: Lloyd E. Nicholson
Manuscript compilation by Ashley Duff

Forward

The Storycatcher Project was initiated by Alexandra Neighbourhood House as part of a larger outreach initiative to older LGBTQ+ adults, called *Sharing our Journeys*. The goal of the initiative is to reduce the social isolation of older queer-identified people, through increasing social contact and civic participation. In doing so, we have had a particular focus on stimulating intergenerational connections between youth and elders – primarily through a six-part discussion series called *Journeying Together*.

As a place-based not-for-profit agency, the mission of Alex House is to partner with our neighbours in manifesting activities focused on community engagement and development. Our attention has always been most steadily fixed on those who identify as marginalized or vulnerable since it these people who are in most need of encouragement and opportunities to connect and engage.

In Canada, much has changed for LGBTQ-identified people over the past generation. But isolation still remains a feature of queer life – especially for older adults, and especially for those living south of the Fraser. We want to change that.

The Storycatcher Project has allowed older LGBTQ+ adults to share their stories – with each other, with their loved ones, and with the LGBTQ+ youth who have been integral to *Sharing our Journeys*. I am pleased to have the opportunity to share it with you, as well.

Alexandra Neighbourhood House is grateful to the Peninsula Community Foundation, whose support through the Canada 150 program made this project possible. My thanks also to the editor of this anthology, Ron Kearse; and to the courageous men and women who have chosen to share their own journeys with us, for posterity.

Neil Fernyhough
Manager, Community Programs
Alexandra Neighbourhood House

Photo credit: Neil Fernyhough

Introduction

George Santayana once said: *Those who cannot remember the past are condemned to repeat it.* That is especially true when it comes to the experiences of our Queer Elders. In these dark times, the voices of the Queer Men, Women and Trans pioneers who are still among us, must be heard. Not only as the voices of our community elders but as living examples of having the courage to overcome inner fears and stand up, sometimes alone, to the virulence of a fearful society. In the 1960s and '70s, we in the Queer community fought for our rights. In the 1980s and early '90s, we fought for our lives, and too many of us are no longer here to bear witness to those times.

But thankfully, those of us who are still here, remember. We remember what it was like to dance in joy along with the Gay Liberation Movement. We remember being pelted with eggs and tomatoes while marching in Pride Parades, which at that time were acts of civil disobedience. We remember the regular assaults and the non-action by police departments to them. In fact, the police were, many time complicit, especially in raids on our bars and bathhouses. We remember lobbying politicians, protesting, setting up community newspapers, radio and television shows. We remember attending too many funerals of our friends, loved ones and peers who passed way too young. We remember standing up to the cynical media, hostile politicians and religious leaders who would sooner have us die than risk votes, their careers and power!

The stories in this anthology are of the pain and ridicule of being different, courage in the face of ostracism, of same-sex love when it was illegal. Until 1969, homosexuality was illegal in Canada, punishable by serving up to two years' in prison.

These are some of the Queer Pioneers who lived through these times and are still around to tell their stories. Of horrible fear in the gay community during the 1980s when AIDS and more so, the *fear* of AIDS killed so many young gay men. And most of all, these are stories of finding the courage to be the person you are. To stand up and be counted. To inspire the Queer Community, and indeed everyone, to be courageous and make their own marks in the world.

These are stories of love, bravery, solidarity and ownership over our own lives! These are the stories of rage, of visibility, of calling out the BS of the status quo, of not giving up the fight for who we are. And if I may offer a twist on the much-loved chant from Queer Nation: We're *still* here; we're *still* Queer! Get used to it!

Ron Kearse
Editor

Ron Kearse

Ron Kearse has been writing all of his life and considers it, *his perfect form of expression*. He's a writer, author, broadcaster, photographer and artist. Work-wise, Ron has had many diverse jobs: from working on a tree farm in Northern Ontario to various Marketing departments, to working with First Nations Offenders in the federal penal system in British Columbia. He enjoys travelling, music, art, photography, being social and is presently learning Spanish and taking guitar lessons. He has much respect for his Celtic, First Nations and Germanic family roots, and at age sixty, he feels life has only begun.

Photo credit: Neil Brock

Table of Contents

Tom Dekker

Tom Dekker has worn several interesting hats throughout his life – musician, self-help and assistive tech advocate and instructor, interface accessibility/usability tester, vision rehab instructor and independent living skills coach.

In the post-DayJob era aka "retirement," Tom has turned his attention to creating online multi-media instructional resources that demonstrate and promote inclusive design. He sees online entrepreneurialism as a powerful alternative and antidote against the plague of marginalization still faced by people with special needs or challenges, as they try to enter the world of more traditional mainstream employment.

Thankfully, as awareness and enlightenment slowly begin to spread through major corporations (starting with Apple), this situation is beginning to improve significantly, though socially and attitudinally, there's still a long way to go.

Tom has worked in Toronto and Ottawa, plus seven years in the US (five in NYC, two in Houston). During this time he worked with several agencies that sent him travelling to more than a dozen cities across the country.

Now he is happy just to work from his beach-front home in Victoria, being entrepreneurial with partner, Ken, fiddling with audio and music production equipment, and playing a little gig here and there.

Photo credit: Ron Kearse

Sound and Furry

For as long as I can remember, furry things always put me in a happy mood. First, it was furry kittens, furry puppies, Mummy's long hair, furry arms of dad and uncles. And later there was hopping in bed with Daddy for underpants-only hugs. Then came summers up at the cottage - all sorts of frisky horseplay and wrestling about.

This was especially true in the water, where there was, it turns out, much fur to be discovered! And what's more, some of these woofderful manimals had much deeper voices and way more fur than Dad!

The coolest thing was that, as a little blind kid, I could feel the fur all I wanted. Nobody cared. After all, I couldn't see. Nothing like leveraging stereotype perceptions! The first boundary came when I attempted to see if the fur carried on below the bathing suit waistline and being told: "That's Not Nice to do!" I didn't quite understand why, but, well OK. But if anything, the idea of "not nice" only fuelled my curiosity!

My great love of fur came an increasing attraction to deep, growly voices and sounds. The chance to wrestle or play tug-of-war with big furry dogs always got me excited in a joyful sort of way. Dogs have always been my good friends. They know a woof-person when they meet one!

No wonder I got interested in wrestling during high school! All that body contact! Plus, there would inadvertently a certain amount of grunting and growly emanations during the matches.

Part of me knew this was all ordinary and "normal," but I was also aware that I was different. I caught enough conversation about certain things that it's "bad for men to do" that I just kept quiet. I didn't seriously believe that such imaginings were bad at all. Somehow, I had a sense this was to do with coming from a smaller town, and that I would eventually find "my kind of normal" in a bigger city. As a result, I was known to often go on about not being able to wait until I could leave home for the big city. And yeah, I did this from a far younger age than I think is usual. Maybe like, about age 6! And why, you may ask? Bigger cities we visited had more stereo rock music stations. I would actually cry when it was time to come back home to an FM dial with two Muzak-spewing "square" stations. I know, audio-tactile priorities! Fur, bottom end bass riffs, rockin' rhythms, and oh! deep voices with interesting foreign accents, particularly southern American and British.

This sort of orientation isn't surprising for a person who has no visual idea of what people actually "look like," or how facial expressions actually work. The concept of "you should've seen the look..." has always had zero significance to me.

But my first bit of coming out was quite odd, simply because my only clue to gayness, or so I perceived, occurred within an audio-only frame of reference. This was mostly triggered (and not in a positive way) by effeminate, lispy voices coming from guys, who seemed to wish they were girls. It took me a long time to sort myself out. I didn't know what I was, but I knew for sure that I was a guy who liked other guys. It had nothing to do with women in any way, shape or form. I liked men who were men. I had some physical fun with a few women. It just never occurred to me to fall in love with them. Besides, women weren't furry. Hell, at one point in contemplating sexual labels, it occurred to me, that had I ever encountered a tall, hefty, furry bearded female who had decided to make me her "daddy," well, I'd essentially have "gone straight." So much for labels!

It also didn't take long for me to figure out that 95% of human interaction is based on "eye contact." This goes double for anything to do with sex, and double again for any interaction considered "abnormal." And "normal" then was much, much narrower than it is now.

Therefore, during my late adolescence (after leaving the blind school), through my 20's and early 30s, I perceived myself as largely out of the game. How could you meet your "type" or even select potential new friends? Without any concept of who's even around you, it's challenging to say the least, especially with loud music, crowd noise, etc. No wonder it was all so visual with yelling required for conversation.

Thankfully, with an increase in self-confidence, I began to realize that I could actually leverage my difference. It was like, "Hey! If you're interested enough, you'll damn well leave your comfort zone and make contact. And if not, then fine! Thanks for saving me a waste of time and energy". Guess what! I met more people from then on. Apparently "confident equals more approachable." Good thing to know!

My increasing confidence also raised the smartass factor, and I started to get cheekier. For example, I'll always remember walking down the street with a friend, having forgotten my white cane, when some idiot yelled: "So are you blind, or queer, or what?" I simply replied, "Both! Now mind your fuckin' business!" Well, apparently, we left him standing there, frozen in indecision, with a totally confused look on his face. Maybe he's still there, trying to figure out whether he should have helped the blind person or punched out the faggot!

Then there's being asked, on multiple occasions when in a bar: "Do you go home with people?" I developed stock answers like: "No, I'm a permanent fixture!" or "If you take me to the pay phone, I'll call my mom and ask if it's OK!"

Anyway, back in 1971, the Toronto gay scene, as far as I knew, consisted of a social group called The Toronto Homophile Association, which, appeared to attract mostly feminine men which didn't interest me; and a couple of bars, the Parkside and St. Charles, which were full of smokers who drank too much and didn't mesh at all with the hippy-type musicians that I liked to hang with. So, I didn't bother going out a lot at that time.

It wasn't until the late 70s that I made a few masculine gay friends and began hanging out at The Barn, the local leather and denim bar at that time. The venue had carpeted floors, which made it easier for me to hear what was going on around me. Then, by the beginning of the 1980s, hard surfaces, bad acoustics and disco became the order of the day, so once again, I lost interest in the gay scene. But at least there was the Toolbox, which played great music and attracted a much more masculine crowd, even if a lot of them were way too kinky for vanilla huggy-woof me.

At about this time, technology became my friend in a new and completely unexpected way, as I found myself ushered through the gateway to the first-ever realm of "CyBearSpace." This came in the form of good old CompuServe, for six US bucks per hour. You wanna see first-time addiction run up a hell of a bill, given the fact that doing it all with a refreshable electronic braille display was really quite slow. But I didn't care. It was worth it! It was inevitable that my attraction to fur and bass, in combination with my socially curious sniffer, would lead me to a community of "bears," or at least, guys who would come to identify as such, as the eighties marched on. I never imagined that my process would ever be so "technologically enhanced"!

The values held by the Bear community were somehow different in a way that considerably minimized the importance of eye contact, especially online, where there was none! Who knew I couldn't see? So, people were friendlier, and I thus got well known at bear events as CaptainWoof, which was particularly effective, especially once people learned of the trusty guide dog at my side, it was just cool, that's all. And of course, dogs are always great ice-breakers!

But my premier personally created bear event was organized through the free pre-www newsgroup called alt.soc.motss (Alternative.Social.members-of-same-sex) in 1991. It didn't cost anything to be sociable there, and my efforts culminated in the arrival at our house of 25 bears from all around the north-east, to party, mostly in the nude, for a long and woofderful weekend! The straight bikers next door didn't know what the hell to make of it since quite a few of the guests were themselves big biker bears. The main event of the weekend was Captain Woof leading a bear tour through downtown Toronto and the Church Street village! And the fur! Oh! The fur of that weekend will live in my memory FUR-ever!

It was official! CyBearSpace could indeed prove a fine alternative to eye contact. It got me an ultimate king sized grizzly papa-bear who took me with him to Montana and Australia, a bear who loved me dearly for four years in NYC before the poor thing died, and, since the end of March, 2003 the amazing bear whose "Folded In Thirds" story appears elsewhere in this book. A pretty effective and successful system, don't you think!

So now, I'm just a furry-faced older, but still middle-aged, woofie-bear person, woofing along with Abe, aka The AbraHound, Seeing Eye dog number six. We started with Woof One in 1977, but unfortunately, these dear creatures don't last anywhere near as long as we would hope. There's always a sad time - dog transition - usually less dramatic though, thanks to understanding and support from friends, family and bearPals. And in general, I've been very fortunate to have many life-long friends for whom sexual preference has never been an issue.

For example, during much of the 70s when I was a travelling rock musician, I was always able to leverage one particular gay stereotype, which seemed to promote the idea that "a lot of keyboard players are queer." While the straight guys found this annoying, I loved it, especially with our straight, sighted drummer who was only too happy to position me for conversation with guys who would keep giving me the eye when we were on stage. See what I mean about supportive straight friends?

Ultimately, NYC was my favourite place for bears, and quite a few became good friends. I began attending what were called, the "Bear Hugs"! Great gatherings of big, furry, friendly creatures, where everybody left their clothes at the door. These happened once a month, and I missed very few of them during my five years living there! Truly a furry, growly bear-adise during each visit! The fond memories will last as long as I do. This is a good thing since most of my NYC Bear Pals are no longer with us. I guess it's a good thing to be a bit vanilla and kind of old-fashioned, or else I might be gone too.

Oh well, what's that old saying? "Once a king, always a king, but once a knight's enough"? After a certain age, it's more like "Once a week's enough." Let's face it! It takes me a week to charge up again. But that's OK. Surprisingly, age-related decline of libido actually leads to much greater peace of mind and inner calm. Quality over quantity becomes the natural order of the day, with an openness to meeting new friends, including a nice huggy-bear here and there. It's much easier to go with the flow and see what the Universe sends our way. I'm grateful for how things have turned out, and how they seem to be unfolding. That's FUR sure!

-Tom Dekker

Fernando Esté

Drawing from various schools and spiritual traditions, Fernando Esté is a Spiritual Director, a Truth-seeker with a life-long experience in social justice and mysticism. Fernando constantly dances between the Wisdom traditions of the world and is an Engineer, Librarian, Zen and Dru Yoga practitioner, who studies, writes, teaches, and shares the joy of living by facilitating and assisting individuals with finding their unique expression of spirituality and creativity through the ancient Universal practice of Spiritual Companioning.

Fernando is also an active member of the Vancouver Sisters of Perpetual Indulgence as Sister Petunia Encarnata, committed to promulgate universal joy, expiate stigmatic guilt, and serve the beloved community. He is a Venezuelan American Canadian living in Vancouver, British Columbia, with Don, his partner since 1999, and Elvis, their beloved Chihuahua.

Photo credit: Ron Kearse

In Search of Authentic Queer Spirituality

Living as a fag teenager in the Caracas of the 60s and 70s was not an easy task, especially when I found myself thrown into emptiness, which plunged me to despair of the purest form. I didn't plan it; it just happened without any preparation on how to survive this emotional and psychological hell. The confusion and mess in which I found myself led to a happy ending, much happier than I ever imagined. That's why I am compelled to write this story, hoping that somehow this experience will assist you in searching for the pearl of great price in your life.

This pearl is given at birth, and it is hidden from view. Once we find it, its inherent magic gift flows from within like a river, equipping you with the essential tools and resources for living a full and abundant life. There are no recipes for the journey, only general guidelines and principles, which I like to call *pointers*.

This *journey into oneself* is the easiest way for me to define spirituality in human terms. But spirituality is much more than that. You may ask yourself, queer spirituality? Really?? Why do we need anything as obscure and senseless as spirituality in our lives? Because life is a Mystery. Because there are no books, big or small, sacred or secular in the entire world or material universe, that could cover all of the things that humans are interested in. Because we are creatures who hunger and thirst for everything; our curiosity and creativity are infinite.

Have you asked yourself questions such as: Where do I come from? Where am I going? What am I doing on this planet? Why are we born? Why do we die? I did. And because I couldn't find any answers that made any sense to me, I was thrown into a journey of despair...which almost killed me. These questions were HUGE for me, and I was ready to face anything and search everywhere to find my answers.

In Psychology Today's Online article, Larry Culliford states: *"spirituality is like an adventure park waiting to be explored...It is not an ideal to consider spirituality as a thing; an object....it is better thought of as a boundary-less dimension of human experience. As such, it must be admitted; it is not open to the normal methodologies of scientific investigation. It cannot completely be defined. It cannot be pinned down. So... What are we to do?"[1]*

So, the door is completely open to the wide, almost infinite variety of human experiences. He continues:

"Firstly, you don't have to give up! You don't have to be like people who equate spirituality with a religion [2] they decide is false, then abandon. It is possible to look at spirituality another way, as something free of institutional structures and hierarchies, not so much about dogma and beliefs as about attitudes, values and practices, about what motivates you (us) at the deepest level, influencing how you think and behave, helping you find a true

and useful place in your community, culture and in the world."

In the last decade, you may have heard people say: *"I am spiritual but not religious."[3]* This statement seems to strike a chord with lots of people who are trying to rescue spirituality from traditional religions. Control over spirituality or spiritual matters has led society, some religious groups and most religious traditions to fail our LGBTQ community. Persecution, demonization, hatred, and sometimes torturing and killing our brothers and sisters throughout the world are still prevalent to this very day.

No wonder LGBTQ folks are more likely to commit suicide and live their lives riddled with addictions and overwhelmed by self-destruction. Where do we find Love? How do we learn what Love is? This is where one of the aspects of being human comes into play: Spirituality. And because this is such a broad terminology, we are going to refer to it here as *Queer Spirituality.*

"There is a really deep well inside me. And in it dwells G_d. Sometimes I am there too. But more often stones and grit block the well, and G_d is buried beneath. Then, (S)He must be dug out again". [4] As indicated elsewhere here in this text, this pearl of great price, our own inherited Wisdom of old, is buried deep inside us. And G_d dwells there...there's work to do to cleanse "the doors of perception...and then everything will appear to us as it is – infinite. In these doors of perception are

trapped cobwebs of thought, prejudice, cowardice, sloth...Eternity is with us, inviting our contemplation perpetually, but we are too arrogant to still our thought and let divine sensation have its way..."[5]

This life-long cleansing operation, my dear young reader, is what *I* call *spirituality*.

To make it really simple, I am going to equate Spirituality with Mystery and Silence. Something that we have a sense of but cannot define. I hope to lead you to a place where you can begin or continue to practice spirituality.

"The purpose of any spiritual practice is to keep us engaged and in dialogue with the Divine, wherever we perceive it, and however we have learned to speak and listen."[6]

How do you define your spirituality? Why is it important to you?

Young folks of the 21st century would benefit tremendously from the Wisdom of the Elders. Wisdom is an acquired capacity, virtue, or ability to process information beyond data collection, reading, and critical thinking, which transforms these into life-giving and embodied experiences useful to live an abundant and happy life. This Wisdom is inside you, it belongs to you, *but it has to grow.* The more your inner Wisdom grows, the more fully human you become. It finds its delight and dwelling places in the heart of humanity. Life as a queer person is wonderful. Filled with possibility and creativity. Joy and sorrow, light and darkness...all are ingredients of this wonderful stew named human experience.

Before you question my assertion, let me say that I do not claim to be a special human being. I have lived in two continents -- half my life in each. I am a Canadian immigrant and a Hispanic, and Spanish is my mother language. Both North and South America have been my home for almost 60 years of happy existence as one of the most screaming and proud faggots my country of origin has ever seen. I wouldn't change the fact that I am a faggot, even if I had the power to live my life all over again.

How did I get here from a place of despair and darkness in my adolescent years? What did I do that led me to this point where I can say that life itself is the most wonderful and awesome adventure?

Well, nothing other than receiving what was given to me. Not having a clue of what was happening to me, other than what I later learned was an unusual awakening event or, to use traditional Christian terminology, *a rare "spiritual" experience*. It was also physical. Fully and wholly physical, which rendered me unto a higher state of consciousness, which, the closest state I can think of is drunkenness or high in the Spirit. I got high in Love.

In the summer of 1975 and I was travelling through Europe after my high school graduation. I visited ten countries, including Italy. I mention Italy because it was in a small Italian city that my life was deeply touched and transformed in an instant by something or someone, whose true nature to this very day remains a Mystery.

We landed in Assisi, the town where one of the world's most popular saints, Saint Francis, was born in 1181. The tour included the Basilica where the remains of the saint are kept in the belly of the Cathedral. As I was contemplating the simplicity of the tomb and its surroundings, I fell on my knees to pray out of respect and devotion. As I prayed, slowly reciting the Lord's Prayer word by word in perfect stillness, I felt like I was transported to heaven in a split second. Consumed by love, which felt like blazing heat burning at the centre of my chest, accompanied by waves of love, which pierced my heart with the healing sweetness of warmth, peace, joy, and calm so deep that tears started flowing down my face.

Without having a clear idea of what was happening, I remember I got up and looked for a priest, to no avail. The need to speak with the Franciscan friars and to beg them to let me stay was overwhelming. Still, in this state of surrender and submission to Love, I followed the tour guide again to the bus, which took us to the next destination. I made sure my journal entry that day reflected what happened in that basilica. I keep a copy of that handwritten journal entry on a piece of paper after 43 years. I think it will be buried with me as a testimony of what really happened that blessed day.

The impact of this event has never been forgotten, and the interpretation, as well as its significance, will continue to enfold the Mystery of Presence of G_d in my life till my last breath. Soon after, it would be revealed to me the purpose of that singular "visitation" was precisely to keep me from committing suicide when all hope, meaning, and appreciation of life were removed from me, leaving me in a state of consciousness close to what I now call *obsessive-compulsive death desire syndrome*. It does not exist in the diagnostic books of mental illness, but I experienced as the reality and evidence of hell on earth which I mentioned earlier.

These types of mystical experiences are not the important thing in our journey. I believe they nurture and sustain us while we walk on Earth as a useful and transformative tool to live a life of compassion and service to others through work. I think my experience happened because it was needed. I was at serious risk of committing suicide as a result of my psychological despair. It was like being taken to the ER hoping that the treatment would restore health and wholesomeness in the midst of a congestive heart failure or a stroke. The healing treatment was of such Nature that I not only was declared healed and released from the hospital, but I did not have to go back ever again to the ER.

In my world, Mysticism and Spirituality are intimately related. I hesitate to insist in or advocate for any rules around spirituality because the moment we create rules, we then are advancing religion, which is not a bad thing, but it has its own problems of politics, corruption, and oppression. I do believe there are signs and results of authentic and healthy spirituality, just like there are signs and results of authentic and healthy lives. Humans have an amazing capacity to create/build wonderful things and yet obliterate/destroy/damage everything we touch. This capacity is also extended to spirituality, which can also be subject to corruption and human error. How do you know whether your spirituality is healthy and life-giving? I would suggest you seek the help of a spiritual companion, who would walk with you, side by side, without judging, assessing, comparing, or trying to fix you.

Yet I know that within each and every being, there is a spark of the Divine. We, humans, hold a beautiful place of great responsibility, wherein we have become the consciousness of the Universe, who reflects upon itself and is capable of great things. Science can assist us in this journey to infinite knowledge and Wisdom but also suffers from human corruption.

I recently learned the suicide index among teenagers has doubled or tripled since 2011, the year when the smartphone industries launched the most aggressive campaign to sell them across North America and Europe. Thus, replacing human contact by human-machine interaction under the illusion that we have virtual "friends" who care about us, rendering us empty and dissatisfied. I have also become aware of a trend of unkindness, passive-aggression, and selfishness in the general population – me included—which leads me to believe there is something inherently wrong in the direction we are going. This trend has not been with us humans in our 50,000 years of evolution, and the full impact on our humanity is still relatively unknown. It has been, slowly but surely, replacing years of storytelling and face to face conversation.

The complexities of human existence are at an all-time peak in 21st century North America. The problems of climate change and overpopulation, environmental crisis, pollution and unsustainability, terrorism, bullying, war, famine, and the like are becoming too big for younger minds to handle emotionally and cognitively. How can they cope? What can save them from despair, depression, and anxiety?

I strongly believe these spirituality principles should be included in the curriculum available in public schools; it may save many lives. Another good place to start is having LGBTQ2S+ spirituality circles, something that I might suggest to our LGBT leaders and community organizers, such as the Sisters of Perpetual Indulgence, Radical Faeries and Q-munity, among other groups.

What would be a good place for a young person to start their journey into themselves and to communities, a place where love and compassion abides deep within ourselves? What would it take for wise elders who are masters in spirituality, from all traditions, to make themselves available and share their stories of struggle and life-giving situations in face to face interactions? These are questions that go beyond our LGBTQ2S+ community, and this is something where queer folks could assist. Look closer at the 2 Spirited Traditions of the First Nations[7].... which was almost wiped out by colonialism, toxic enculturation and abuse on the part of the European culture, plagued with homophobia and misogyny. My understanding of these 2S Traditions is they were healers and were considered sacred by most cultures. I am not an expert in these matters, but I want to mention that we have a strong presence among ancient cultures in North America. Books are always good reference sources, and your public library can be extremely helpful in finding excellent reading material[8].

-Fernando Esté

---

[1] Culliford, Larry. Psychology Today online: https://www.psychologytoday.com/blog/spiritual-wisdom-secular-times/201103/what-is-spirituality. As it appears on November 27, 2017.
[2] See https://www.psychologytoday.com/basics/religion
[3] See https://www.psychologytoday.com/blog/rationally-speaking/201007/spiritual-not-religious
[4] Etty Hillesum, An Interrupted Life.
[5] Evelyn Underhill, Practical Mysticism
[6] Baldwin, Christina. The Seven Whispers, New World Library, Novato California. 2002, p.15
[7] https://en.wikipedia.org/wiki/Two-spirit
[8] For instance, check A Two-Spirit Journey: The Autobiography of a lesbian Ojibwa-Cree Elder by Ma-Nee Chacaby, Winnipeg, Manitoba, UMP, 2016, at the Vancouver Public Library.

Ken Sudhues

A fourth-generation Victorian, Ken has lived in Gibsons, Ottawa and Toronto before finally returning home to stay in 2014. He's been out pretty much forever, which made high school and university in the 70s "interesting" if nothing else.

Ken has worked in radio and the public service, with many years spent at health ministries in BC and Ontario. He is now a partner in iHabilitation Canada, a company that assists blind touch-screen users, with his spouse, Tom Dekker.

Having separated in 2007, due to increasing dementia and need for care, David Nixon, the subject of Ken's story, was his spouse from 1978 until David's death in 2017.

There is a lot more to David's incredible life than will fit in a single chapter. Anyone who wishes to go deeper is invited to check out Ken's blog on Wordpress.com, OurMisterNixon. It contains David's letters, oodles of selected photos and slides, and much more.

Photo credit: Ron Kearse

A Life, Folded in Thirds

It was a hot and sunny August afternoon in 1978, the kind of day that makes Victoria pretty close to paradise. After living away for a few years I was home, hanging out with friends, smoking lots of other people's weed, and wallowing in the joy of summer.

My friend Laura told me I really needed to meet her godfather, David Nixon. "Well," she said, "he's not my real godfather, but he's really interesting. He's lived all over the world, has a really cool apartment on a hill... oh, and he's gay, too. You'll like him."

Laura, her boyfriend (a supplier of excellent weed), and I rolled up to David's place, and there he was. Considerably older than me, average height and weight, bald, but furry everywhere – and with a full beard. This was my kind of man!

The four of us spent the afternoon lying around on David's "nests" – huge foam filled corduroy bags that conformed to whatever shape you wanted them to – talking, toking, drinking wine and generally getting wasted amid a jungle of houseplants, art and bric-a-brac. It was wonderful!

Eventually, Laura and her beau decided it was time to depart, but David told me I was welcome to stay. He didn't have to ask me twice! With both an active libido and daddy-ish tendencies, he was just what I needed. I was 22, and he was almost 44 – twice my age, but really cool for an old guy! Little did I know this was the beginning of a very long relationship.

As things progressed, I learned a lot about David and the life he'd led. It turned out to be the most amazingly wild mixture of fun, adventure, horror, recovery, then more adventure.

David came from an odd family. He and his older brother were late arrivals in their parents' marriage. Such was the state of medicine in the 1930s that his brother was first diagnosed as an ulcer and David as appendicitis. After graduating from Ottawa's High School of Commerce in 1952, David found work with the federal government, and by 1954, he was with the Department of Foreign Affairs.

Meanwhile, in what was then French Indochina, there waged a messy war. The French were fighting to hold onto their colonies of Viet Nam, Laos and Cambodia, but it was hopeless. The United Nations formed an International Supervisory Commission to monitor the transition to independence. The commission was made up of military and diplomatic representatives from India, Poland, and Canada.

Back then, one had to be at least 25 to be sent overseas with Foreign Affairs, but Indochina was considered a war zone, so no women could be sent to do the clerical work. David, with his excellent shorthand, bookkeeping and clerical skills was offered the job of office clerk in Phnom Penh, Cambodia, at the age of 19. After eagerly accepting the offer, David's first response was to find a world globe to see where the hell Phnom Penh was!

In the age of air travel before passenger jets, getting to the other side of the world took a long time. In early September 1954, David flew from Ottawa to Tokyo via Toronto, Winnipeg, Vancouver, and Adak (Alaska). After three days of briefings and other preparations, he then flew from Tokyo to Phnom Penh via Okinawa, Hong Kong, and Hanoi.

As David's story unfolded, I found he had an interesting habit of turning up in the wrong places but at the right time. For instance, Indochina between the departure of the French and arrival of the Americans was relatively calm, so David and his military buddies had ample time to act like tourists. David's long letters home (which his family saved) are full of giddy accounts of side-trips to the Gulf of Siam, Saigon, and, best of all, Angkor. He was able to spend three days on a guided tour of the ruins of Angkor with a very small group and no other tourists. Because of the recent unrest, there were no other visitors. They had Angkor to themselves.

David was also a very good photographer and took pictures as well as slides. The photos are all in black & white, standard for that time, but the slides are in colour. His collection is breathtaking, and what he had seen, he showed me.

During this time, David said that he was still trying to figure himself out. His attraction to other men was there, but in the particular situation and political climate, there was no way to act on it.

After several months in Cambodia, where he turned 20 and grew his first decent mustache, David's term ended, and he returned to Canada, but not for long. Next stop, Germany. To be exact, the city of Bonn, capital of West Germany, in the middle of the Cold War.

The government's preferred option to cross the Atlantic was by ship. David was duly packed off to Europe, wide-eyed and still mostly innocent, in first class on an ocean liner. He said it was like travelling in an old Hollywood movie, only in colour!

Europe in the 1950s was still recovering from a major war; borders not yet fixed, refugees still being placed, massive rebuilding underway and the so-called Iron Curtain becoming a hard reality. West Germany was in the midst of everything, and Canada's role was larger than most people realized at the time.

David started as an office clerk in the Canadian Embassy but soon found himself promoted to the communications section where he became a cryptographer, coding and decoding sensitive documents. Over time, his security clearance rose to where he handled many documents that were dictated to him by the ambassador, coded, and sent to Ottawa, where they were decoded and handed to either the minister of Foreign Affairs or the prime minister.

Despite the world-shaking events taking place across the continent during David's tenure (1955-59), there was always time for fun, travel, and romance. David's best friend, Sylvia Tysick, made a name for herself as a dancer and actress and moved to London in 1957. David travelled to London regularly and saw lots of shows in the West End, including Sylvia's.

David and Sylvia were ideal travel companions and drove all over western Europe in David's 1951 VW Beetle. Paris, Amsterdam, Geneva, Venice, they saw the lot, and did all the touristy things that one did back then.

And there was romance. David had his first real relationship in Bonn, with a man named George, who also worked in the embassy. George was bisexual but gave David all his attention. He was apparently "gifted," too. David's nickname for him was Basket Balls.

The next big adventure for Mr. Nixon was in Africa. He was sent to the new embassy in what was then Leopoldville (Kinshasa) in what had only recently been the Belgian Congo. Again, David was in what many considered to be a terribly dangerous place, especially for white people. It was dangerous for David, too, but he got through it. One day, driving home for lunch, he was stopped at a roadblock set up by provisional government troops, noted for being short on patience and quick on the trigger. On reaching for his diplomatic passport, he realized it was still sitting on his desk. Gulp. Searching his wallet, David produced the only official-looking things he could: his Congo driver's permit and his Ontario liquor license (back then, you had to have an actual license to buy liquor in Ontario!). After careful inspection of both items, he was saluted and waved through.

The Congo was David's last posting. In reading his letters and looking at photos, it was fairly apparent that he was seeing a couple of men from other embassies. On applying for leave to take a holiday in early 1962, he was instead ordered back to Ottawa pronto. A few days after returning to his post there, he was invited to an "interview" with the RCMP.

As David told the story, it was late afternoon, and he was shown into an office facing a man at a desk in front of a west-facing window. The blinds were angled so that the sun was directly in David's eyes, keeping the occupant of the desk in silhouette. From behind the desk came, "We have reason to believe that you are a homosexual. As such, you are a security risk and must be removed from the civil service. You have the option of resigning your position immediately, or we will see to it that you are removed."

With that, David's career with the diplomatic corps was over.

Unable to find meaningful work without references from Foreign Affairs and unable to discuss the reasons for his sudden departure from the civil service, David moved to London, then to Montreal in the hope that a change of scene and culture could help him start over. Already in a deep depression, David's mood only worsened. He finally sought medical attention and was referred to a psychiatrist. That psychiatrist, in turn, referred him to a clinic at the Allan Memorial Institute.

Sometime after being admitted to "the Allan," David came to the attention of its director, Dr. D. Ewen Cameron, who was working for the RCMP and the American CIA, using combinations of drugs and other treatment to effect behavioural changes in patients. David underwent at least 36 grand-mal electroconvulsive (shock) treatments in quick succession and was prescribed large doses of drugs including Seconal.

This particular phase of David's life, even the timing of his admission and treatment, remained indistinct for him for many years. The only things he was sure about was that he had checked himself in sometime in 1963 and checked himself out – against the wishes of those running the clinic – sometime in late 1964. David recalled that he left the Allan feeling "blank." He had little recollection of where he had been, who his friends were, where he had worked – it was all pretty much gone. Only by talking to his family and the friends he could remember, reading his letters from overseas, and looking through his photos and slides, could David reassemble some memory of his past life.

David remained positive, though. He turned 30 in December 1964, officially old in his eyes. To celebrate that and surviving the Allan, our Mr. Nixon did what he enjoyed most. He packed his bag and went travelling again.

Postscript:

Whatever treatment he'd received at the Allan achieved some level of security for the government: David said that every time he tried to visualize the cipher machines or codebooks he'd used, it was as if a hand pushed him away and he could never see them for more than a fraction of a second before being "redirected".

In the late 1980's, the federal government offered a compensation package to those who had been affected by Dr. Cameron's treatments. David wrote to the Allan for a copy of his file. Several hundred pages of photocopies arrived soon after with a note saying that these were just David's clinic records. All Dr. Cameron's records had been destroyed – by him – shortly before his death. David's doctor read through the file, noting the numbers and strength of the drugs given. He then shook David's hand and congratulated him on still being alive.

As it turned out, David didn't qualify for the compensation package – he wasn't damaged badly enough, but obtaining his file from the Allan at least gave him firm dates about his admission and release, allowing him to put a few more pieces in the puzzle of his earlier life.

And the reference "folded in thirds" in the title? David always said that the only way to fold laundry efficiently was in thirds – shirts, underwear, towels, etc. He said that his life had been folded in thirds, too: before Montreal, Montreal, and, finally, Victoria.

David Nixon died in February 2017, after a 17-year decline with dementia.

-Ken Sudhues

Cyndia Cole

Cyndia Cole moved from the USA to Vancouver in 1970 and came out as a lesbian at 26 in 1976. Her writing appears in *Basically Queer: An Intergenerational Introduction to LGBTQA2S+ Lives, Making Room: Forty Years of Room Magazine* and *Breakthrough*. Daisaku Ikeda taught her that words change people's hearts. She is honoured to have worked with others to found or develop: Women's Studies at SFU, Vancouver East Housing Co-op, humanistic Home Support, Quirk-e, QMUNITY and SGI Vancouver Buddhist Pride Group.

Photo credit: Angie Joyce

Photo credit: Judy Fletcher

That's What Friends Are For

I first met Bill Morrow in December of 1989. We both attended a Palliative Care training day for Community Health Workers in Vancouver. It was a rare treat to be paid for education instead of our daily routine of visiting elderly and disabled clients in their homes. Palliative Care was very focused on end of life comfort care for people with cancer. The training gave scant attention to AIDS which at that time was a considered a scary almost unmentionable topic. Even so, I had already lost my close friend Andrew to this pandemic and had met many of his friends through the Persons with AIDS (PWA) organization.

There were very few men in our field of work, so they really stood out. Almost all took pains to let you know that despite working as caregivers, they were real men, aka heterosexual. Bill was different. He was portly and balding with bushy white eyebrows that marked him as 20 years older than most of us workers. He exuded a warmth and softness that told my gaydar he was part of our rainbow family. For five years I had felt so isolated and vulnerable as a lesbian in-home support. Right away I determined in my heart to get to know Bill. More than the simple desire for a friend and ally in the work arena, I sensed that Bill would somehow play a very significant role in my life. This intuition seemed implausible because Bill worked on the west side while I worked on the east side. Trainings such as this were rare. In this era before electronic transfers, we visited the office every two weeks to pick up our printed schedules and paycheques but only for a few minutes. This was long before Facebook, texting, cell phones or email. How would I ever see Bill again?

Only a month later, in January of 1990, I was accepted for a promotion to supervisor. Since I would no longer be giving hands-on personal care, I would be more protected from the danger that a client would complain about being touched by a lesbian. The risk of losing my job due to homophobia was reduced at least a little. In the two weeks before starting the new job, my east side clients were reassigned, and I was sent to float temporarily with the west side clients. One day I was sent way over near UBC and was asked to take Bill's paycheque with me. I was told "Bill's so busy he can't get to the office to claim it. Leave it at the client's place, and Bill will get it on his next visit there." Interesting, I thought, I won't get to see Bill but will see where he works.

The west side client was a slim fellow in his late twenties and my first with AIDS. He was sweaty and dishevelled but not too wasted looking. He kept his distance curled up on the futon couch clutching a red blanket. I wanted to set him at ease but if I came out to him and he shared it with other workers or the office I could easily be fired. There was no anti-discrimination protection in 1990 and fear was rampant. So I said, "I wonder if you know my friend Kenny who's quite involved with PWA (Persons with AIDS)?" "No," he replied relaxing only a little. "Can I make you a sandwich?" He nodded yes. After I finished, I tried again. His striking blond hair was oily and tangled. "Shall I wash your hair here at the sink?" I could feel how shocked he was that I volunteered to have physical contact with him. My heart ached that people's phobias made him feel untouchable. His protective wall came down as he accepted the nurturing of being cleansed.

I tidied up a bit noticing the unusual way the natural light came in through a line of windows near the ceiling. I looked out at the concrete slabs surrounding a backyard pond and the profusion of native plants in this area of town where British colonial transplants were the standard. Because the small house was placed on the corner of this city lot rather than in the middle, I felt as if we were secluded in the rainforest. Just before I left, I remarked, "What a unique house and garden you have." He tossed off casually, "Oh my partner's an architect, and he built them." "Cool," I smiled, "Don't forget to tell Bill about his paycheque." "I won't. Bill's great, isn't he?" he replied. I wished I could say yes from greater experience.

Years later when I told Bill this story, he said, "Of course the house was special! His partner was

Arthur Erickson. Did you see it featured recently in Vancouver Living Magazine?" My jaw dropped. "You mean I was tidying up the home of a world-famous architect, the one who designed the Museum, the Courthouse and the new University and his partner couldn't even mention his name?" Bill shrugged, "Remember the 'shame' of AIDS."

Our agency began getting more and more referrals to provide personal care to young men with AIDS who were all assumed to be gay. They were such a different population than the elderly we'd been serving. It was hard for me to navigate getting them respectful care without outing myself. We worked in teams of two supervisors. My first work partner was Gail who had been my supervisor before I got promoted. Bill had just been promoted to a supervisor for the West End team. A group of us were chatting in the office when Gail offered, "I've never actually met anyone who's gay." Of course, she'd met me, Bill, Maryanne, Russ, Nina and Karen, about half the office staff she worked with daily. Clearly we were out to each other but not to her. We exchanged awkward glances, but no one said a word. If I risked it by coming out myself, I felt I might compromise my closeted colleagues, harm them and lose their covert support. We had an unspoken code that one must never betray another's trust by outing them without their explicit permission. I, too, chose silence as safer than truth. Even with such numbers not one of us informed Gail of her error.

I learned that Bill's work partner was soon to depart. No one said she was getting fired, but everyone knew that her work was in great disorder and she seemed unable to cope. I quickly asked the boss if I could move sideways to the West End Team and take over her responsibilities. The boss was most relieved to fill the position. Everyone reacted with surprise. I'd been enjoying supervising the East Side team where I'd lived and worked for so long. My co-workers said, "You know the West End team is a mess and that job will be much harder at no extra pay. Why would you want to put yourself through that?" I gave some vague response like, "someone needs to" or "I like a challenge." There was no way I'd share my real reason. "I'll feel so much safer to have Bill as my co-supervisor. I can be myself with him. Together he and I can ensure that the West End gay clients with AIDS are treated without fear and stigma." I thought but never said.

Astonishingly, within six months of meeting Bill and thinking we might never cross paths again, we were sharing a tiny office together for eight hours a day. We were jointly figuring out how to communicate with 25 workers and 200 clients each day and how to untangle the mess. The "much harder" warning of my colleagues was quite accurate. Good thing Bill's easygoing "one day at a time" attitude calmed me down over and over again. His good listening was my reliable de-stressor.

While I stayed in the office to field calls, give directions and make schedules, Bill went out to visit and address problems with the clients and workers. Bill calmed them just like he did me. No one ever felt judged by him, and that smoothed a lot of jagged edges. He wrote reports by hand in triplicate in those pre-computer days then passed them to me. I needed the information but also corrected his spellings and added the last letter to many words. Bill had struggled throughout elementary school due to his dyslexia. By the time he went to BCIT and UBC, he'd learned to cope and work around his learning challenges. He was able to let his great wit and intellect shine. I was just the gentle editor he needed. Bill was also bugged by his lifelong inability to remember names. He quipped often, "I have a good but short memory." Fortunately, memory is my strong suit. And Bill's emotional intelligence was the perfect complement to my organizational skills. We balanced each other at work.

I took the mystic way I'd encountered Bill and become his work partner as evidence of that the deeper rhythms of our lives were aligning for our growth and happiness. This view was based on my daily practice of Buddhism with the SGI (Soka Gakkai International.) I'd been following this life-enhancing philosophy for ten years before I met Bill and used it to transform all the muck I met along the way. I chanted twice daily, went to lots of meetings and became persuaded that we grow through struggle. Even though I eagerly shared this practice with anyone who showed the slightest interest, I naively assumed Bill would not be open to it. Was it an unconscious prejudice that "old white guys" weren't into alternate or Asian based spirituality? So I tried not to talk about Buddhism too much.

However, our philosophy taught that chanting Nam-myoho-renge-kyo even once would have a lasting beneficial effect on someone's life. I certainly wanted only good for Bill. So I plotted how to expose him. I was about to sing with our chorus at a large meeting at the SGI Centre. I figured Bill was such a supportive friend he'd come to see me perform no matter where, so I invited him as a guest. It's ironic that I didn't yet know that Bill described himself as tone deaf. He was never particularly moved by good music nor bothered by music badly done. He never listened to background music, only to talk radio. Despite being indifferent to concerts, Bill did agree to join me that Sunday. To my relief, he seemed comfortable enough with the chanting, speeches and with being in the white minority. We didn't talk about it much afterward. There was always so much about work to communicate. I just assumed he wouldn't want to go again, so I didn't invite him.

About a month later my friend Kenny told me he'd run into Bill by chance near the bus stop. They'd only met once before at that SGI meeting but had connected through their gaydar. According to Kenny, Bill said "When I was a teenager my minister wanted to 'pray the gay away' in front of the whole congregation, I 'fired God' and ran away. I've been searching for an alternative ever since. I've been chanting every day since the first time I heard it and want to commit to it as my ongoing spiritual practice." I was brought up short by my closed-minded assumptions and reluctance to share Buddhism with Bill. I was also astonished that he'd kept this secret from me, given that we spent almost 40 hours a week in close proximity. But then Bill had mastered secrets by being in the closet until he turned

54. He'd had to hide to survive in his jobs that queers were considered uniquely unqualified for – teaching elementary school, being a prison guard, a psychiatric nurse and a social worker. He kept changing jobs due to his unhappiness but never because his gayness was exposed.

Now that Bill and I were bonded as co-workers, queers and Buddhists we shared time together both during and after work. He trusted me with the stories of trauma from his early life, and I marvelled at the well-tempered person he'd become by living through them. We supported each other through the deaths of over 300 gay men with AIDS, as well as those by suicide, heart attack and old age. He helped my partner, and I found the SGI Vancouver Buddhist Pride Group. Year after year Bill spent all day at the SGI booth at the Pride and Stonewall Festivals sharing with anyone who came by. When he retired early due to poor health, he became active in groups for Queer Elders like Quirk-e, Over the Rainbow and Twisted Cooks. He moved into the basement suite at our purple three-story home, Spud Palace and became a treasured member of our chosen family. In sharp contrast to the isolation of many older, single gay men he lived surrounded by love and care until he passed away a month before his 85th birthday. At his Celebration of Life, eighty people joined me in singing the truth I learned from Bill Morrow - "That's What Friends Are For."

-Cyndia Cole

Greta Hurst

On her 80th birthday, she couldn't relate to that age and came up with the "20-year plan." She'd do everything possible she wanted to do and nothing that she didn't want to do or continue with. The best decision proved to be what other people suggested. She expects the next 18 years to be as good as it is today. She's a member of Quirke (the senior queer writing group), as well as other organizations.

Photo credit: Cyndia Cole

My Twenty-Year Plan

I didn't want to celebrate my 80th birthday because I would be acknowledging I was now old! Really? Moi? Old? That was so 'up my nose.' I stewed about that more than a week. Previously, I would do what I wanted and refuse anything I wasn't interested in. However, now that I am older, I would consider doing things that others might suggest. This proved to be a challenge but also proved to be wonderful.

Several months after my new-plan-for-the-rest-of-my-life (god willing, of course), a friend, who was a member of the regional Board of Directors for a group to which I belonged, called to ask if I would consider joining the Board as a Member-At-Large. I was not keen on the idea. In fact, I made some unfriendly comments about what a bad idea that was. Then I remembered that I had committed to trying suggestions from other people. So, a few days later I called her apologizing for our previous phone call and said that I accepted the challenge.

I had checked the Board requirements, which seemed straightforward at the time, but there was no job description. In hindsight, that should have raised concern on my part, but I hadn't given it a second thought. It was later I found out the position required computer skills. When the first computer assignment was given to me, it was clear I couldn't do it. I called another board member telling her my problem, and she said she'd do it. As luck would have it, another computer job was given to me, so I called another board member I felt a good connection with.

I asked her "What shall I do?"

She answered, "No problem, I'll do it."

I started feeling very uneasy. What if this continues for the rest of the term of my position?

Our organization was always being invited to make presentations to other groups. It was part of every board member's job to go in teams of two to every group who invited us, to present a new way of engaging our members to participate more fully in the organization. The chair and I went to Montana and Alaska to present our program to their groups. Both places were new to me which was also exciting because our hosts took us on tours of their local surroundings. I love travelling, and I was being accommodated by a member of the region. It was wonderful to watch how engaged and excited the members were. They came up with ideas of things they'd like to see happen. Being a 'people person' was the highlight of my job.

The "Peter Principle" came to mind that I was operating at a level beyond my capacity which was now upsetting me. I felt I had lost my integrity and decided to discuss this with the Board chair. Although she was kind and somewhat reassuring, I could hardly wait until my term was completed. I wasn't prepared to quit. Two others had quit their positions which was something I couldn't consider.

It was much later I realized these experiences had lasting effects on me. I had become more assertive and felt more connected to people because of my experience as a Board member. I made several changes to my life and felt more confident despite my experience in the past year. I was more comfortable with all sorts of people – men and women and was invited out more often to many other activities that I hadn't done before, including playing games, which I had never done previously. I became an usher at my church (my first church, which I never have considered as fulfilling). I accomplished a long-time wish to visit Haida Gwaii (the Queen Charlotte Islands) with my friend, Sheila. I took the Conscious Girlfriend course on how to improve relationships, both intimate and friendly with new people in my life.

On December 1st, (World Aids Day), I joined a huge number of Canadian Grandmothers, (a project of the Stephen Lewis Foundation), to do a Flash Mob dance at a large Surrey shopping plaza. This was to raise money to finance the African Grandmothers' projects supporting their orphaned grandchildren to feed and school them. It was an amazing experience, all of us in the red shirts of the Grandmothers Campaign doing a synchronized dance. It was a heady experience of me in the front line (of course!), one of, what seemed like, hundreds of red-shirted women dancing to a large audience of shoppers and press filming us. We were on the 6 p.m. news that evening!

Needless to say, I'm taking excellent care of myself with diet, exercise and all the other things I need to do. I have many more plans and adventures because the next eighteen years will go by very quickly. My 82nd birthday is just a few days away.

-Greta Hurst

Brian Baxter

Brian was born and raised in Nova Scotia. He's spent many years here in British Columbia. Back in high school, all the girls loved going out with him because they knew they'd have fun...and they knew they'd be safe.

Photo credit: Skydancer

I Always Knew

I always knew. I think most everyone knew....at least subconsciously. Small town Nova Scotia. Maybe they didn't talk about it. My parents, on occasion, warned me, in their way, to not go down *that* road. I'm not sure whether it was concern for me or for *what-would-the-neighbours-think*. It shows in early photos...not that I was flamboyant, but I was not afraid to let my spirit shine through.

True, homosexuality was misunderstood and therefore frowned on in the '50's.

My elderly neighbours, a Mother and Daughter team, saw me as the sensitive, artistic, nature-loving young boy that I was. They knew I loved birds. On my 10th birthday, they gifted me a budgie. I had to choose the one I wanted. The cage at the Five and Dime was full of green ones and one blue one. I, of course, choose the blue one. I was very excited when I got it home. Then I was told I needed to name it. Even at that age, I knew I wasn't going to call it Blue Boy. I named it Pretty Boy. That should have been a major clue.

When sexual curiosity raised its head, I would play with boys until the word got around that I was playing too earnestly. That, and with increasing comments from my parents, I knew I had to retreat to survive. There were also two known sexual predators around who took advantage of young boys. I had already been approached by both. Another reason to hide. Maybe that's why, in later years, older guys always frightened me.

One of my earliest memories was of my brother, one year and four months older than me, taking me aside and pointing at me said "You are you! I am me!" This was my first understanding of separation. Yet, it also freed me to be myself. Then later I found out that the true nature of myself was not accepted. My true self had to step back and my actor-self stepped forward. (It's no surprise that in Grade 12, I would win best actor in a regional competition of high school theatre).

Another hindrance to being self-aware was that I grew up in a household that still believed children were too young to have worthwhile feelings or intelligence. This created a lifelong anxiety about not being heard.

Girls. I liked them. I could, at that time in my life, be natural and sensitive with them. These qualities didn't go over so well with the boys though. They were being indoctrinated into the world of machismo…brave, strong, and without feelings. I must admit I was a bit shocked when I 'saw' my first naked girl. *There's nothing down there! Kind of like a doll.* When I understood the nature of the mechanics of hetero sex, I was more appreciative.

It was also at this time that the once-disappointing Christmas gift of a set of Encyclopedia Britannica became useful to me. My big, secret, discovery was how much the Romans and Greeks appreciated the male body as much as I did. I loved looking at the sculptures within those pages!

The dichotomy and frustration of those years was that I was not supposed to be interested in boys, but I couldn't date girls until I was 16. I had a few crushes in the Elementary grades, but my first real infatuations happened in High School. Openly with girls, inwardly with boys. My Mother, besides having her own issues of jealousy, was worried I'd get some girl pregnant. Years later the joke was, all the girls I dated had since said they loved going out with me because they knew they'd have fun and they knew they'd be safe! Except for my *best friend* who said that I couldn't see the forest for the trees. She ended up marrying my older brother, who eventually came out as gay too. That story could be a book.

I was brought up in a strict family. Church was a must do, every Sunday, sometimes twice. I'm very familiar with being an altar boy in an Anglican church. I was even teaching bible class to kids when I had already lost my faith in religion. Because of the repressive attitude about sex in my family, I was still a virgin when I left my hometown at 18.

In my first year at Art School, I met a guy who became a full-on crush. Tall, dark, handsome, he had an offbeat sense of humour that I loved. Meanwhile, I was trying my hand at being straight, awkwardly asking young women out on dates and getting a lot of refusals.

By the next summer, still a virgin, I was living at home, working as a lifeguard. One afternoon, lying on my bed listening to an American radio station, I first heard Carly Simon singing *That's the Way I've Always Heard It Should Be*. It haunted me. That song was a call to action. I decided to hitchhike to New Brunswick to surprise my crush. He was surprised but pleased. He was living at home, and his Mother put me up in the back sunroom. It might have seemed innocent on the surface, and I wasn't clear on my motives.

Back at Art School in Halifax, I met his friends, and they became mine. I even invited some of them down one weekend to stay at my parents' cottage. My Mother was beside herself thinking this mixed crowd was having a wild sex weekend. Ha!

It wasn't until one night at my friend's place that things developed under the guise of mutual massage. Having a cock in my mouth gave me the answer. Next day, I met my Mother and sister, and I was afraid that they'd see that I had been sucking cock the night before.

However, that relationship did not last for long. He had issues about being gay and so left town abruptly. He broke my heart with a goodbye letter. I swore off men. And renewed my awkward dating-girls-program.

Meanwhile, my best friend from high school and I were visiting back and forth between Wolfville and Halifax. Eventually, she said that she knew an artistic guy whom she thought I would have a lot in common. Little did she know!

On sunny white winter's day, I hitched down to picturesque Acadia University to meet my best friend and this mystery guy for lunch. I was stunned when I saw him. I was awkward…because I knew he was "the one." (And a year later, I would find out he had seen me walking towards the dining hall, and his reaction was *he's the one for me*). He was very curious about art school. I was very curious about him. My struggle between what I *should* be and who I actually was surfaced again.

Early next September, back at art school for my second year, I was having a late lunch at the Dalhousie SUB. I looked up to see him standing on some nearby steps. Beside him stood a woman who looked like Carly Simon! He saw me almost immediately and made his way to my table. He was now registered for art school.

That autumn, I would see him, occasionally, because we were in different classes. We gradually got to know each other more. Next March he invited me to his room in an 18th-century wood house with huge windows. We had dinner as a blizzard blew into town. I ended up spending the night. I lived miles away, and the city was shut down. But it was an innocent night. I did see him naked. I was afraid he'd see I was very aroused.

I was determined to make next weekend different. I invited him to dinner at my place. I had the house to myself. It was Easter break. We became very intimate, and he spent the night. We then drove down to the Valley. He met my parents and my sister. My mother and sister pulled out all their flirting techniques.

We became intense. I visited him in his hometown, Thunder Bay that summer and met his very accepting family.

The art school had a credited course called World Encounter. The students created their own program, travelled and returned to submit their findings. Even though we would break several 'rules' of the program, we applied. The staff seemed to realize it was our honeymoon and so agreed. Off to Europe, we went for three months.

I learned a lot about art, other cultures and Hugh, and I earned major credits in life.

-Brian Baxter

Claude Hewitt

I have lived in the Vancouver area since 1984 and having travelled extensively, think that there is no better place to call home.

During this time, I have been involved as an active supporter of LGBTQ rights as well as human rights and environmental issues that affect us all.

I am fortunate to have a loving and supportive husband who thinks the same way that I do and this year we will celebrate our 7th wedding anniversary.

I will continue to publically support human rights and environmental issues and hope that by example the younger generations will see the value that speaking out for injustice makes our world a better place.

Photo credit: Ron Kearse

When Life Hands You Lemons

Admitting that I am gay has not always been easy for me. Like a lot of men and women of my generation, it was not talked about in families unless it was with a sneer or a derogatory joke.

Growing up in the 50's, it was something that I was truly unaware existed and never entered my mind. So I remained comfortably ignorant until I was twenty, and then only convinced myself that *a person was a person and body was a body.*

This train of thought coupled with my religious upbringing allowed me to date women and have sex with guys occasionally. Women were taboo for sexual pleasure, as a good Christian you had to wait until you were married. In my twisted way of thinking it was ok to have some fun with guys because someday I would be married and have children and that was going to be my life.

It became more complicated when I found myself becoming attracted to someone for more than sex and that really confused me and thus began my revolving closet door. Finally, at the age of 28, I faced up to the reality that I was a fag, queer and all the other names that had been thrown around between boys when I was growing up.

Facing up to this reality provided several additional problems, the foremost being "coming out" to my family. My youngest sister who is eight years younger was the testing ground. She and I had always been very close and when I got up the courage to tell her that her older brother, who she had always put up on a pedestal, was gay. I was surprised that she accepted it so easily. The rest of my family was kept in the dark for several more years. My father and brother were the hunter-fisherman type, and I thought there would be no way I would ever be able to tell them about my being queer.

My oldest sister who is five years older than me had chosen to follow a religious path, which didn't leave room for tolerance or acceptance, or so I thought. An ex-boyfriend unknowingly outted me to her. He had assumed that she knew and when he told me I freaked out on him. That's what fear does; it takes you to a place where even your friends become targets as a result of your fear.

So in 1984, I made the life-changing decision to move to from Calgary to Vancouver.

Settling into life in Vancouver was what I had expected. But it was a time of great fear as AIDS was hitting the gay community hard. Frail bodies of young men wasting away to a look far beyond their years was frightening. The provincial government consisted of a lot of ultra-right wing, religious, hypocrites who wanted to segregate the men infected and quarantine them on Dead Man's' Island in Stanley Park. Hospitals were segregating AIDS patients into wards with one exception. St Paul's Hospital in Vancouver is at the eastern edge of the *Gay Ghetto* and was run by the Sisters of Providence.

Their compassion allowed for patients, no matter their disease, to be cared for according to their category of illness. Instead of making wards filled with only AIDS patients, they would place those with Pneumocystis in respiratory care, and those with Kaposi Sarcoma into areas with those being treated for other cancers. This simple act of kindness, which provided so much dignity for patients, family and friends, had a great impact on me. It was then I decided that somehow, I would find a way to find employment at St. Paul's. After careful planning and more formal education, I was able to make a career there for twenty years.

When you are young, you believe you are invincible and will live forever. But when you are faced with impending death because you had unprotected anal sex, you begin to analyze your life and look for accomplishments.

I began to think more about the community and less about myself. What was the point of moving here if I was only going to live the life I had moved to get away from? I decided to do some volunteer work. The Vancouver Gay Community Centre was a few blocks from my place and upon enquiring, found they needed help in their library. Being an avid reader at that time, I relished the thought of being able to get my hands on all the queer literature my brain could consume. Much to my surprise, this would later enable me to complete my coming out process to the rest of the as yet untold members of my family.

My oldest sister invited me to her wedding back in Alberta in July of that year, and my mother needed help preparing for the wedding so being the dutiful son I returned to help her out.

During the cutting and wrapping of the wedding cake pieces that would be handed to guests, my mother commented, "someday we will be doing this for you."

I blurted out, "No, I don't think so."

When she asked why not I finally told her the truth. I am homosexual.

She looked at me for a moment and said what I thought was a strange thing, "I didn't know that." Then she asked me another strange thing. "How do you know, have you tried it?" As if being gay was like trying on a shirt to know if you liked it.

We chatted a bit more about when I knew and who else had I told. She was, to my surprise, hurt that both my sisters had known for years and I hadn't told her before. I told her that I thought her religion wouldn't have allowed her to understand and accept me. She told me she loved me and that I was her son.

At that moment, the front door was opening, and she exclaimed, "that's your father, don't say anything to him; he wouldn't understand. I'll tell him."

It was the end of the conversation. We both went on to make small talk with my dad. Was I doing the right thing by not sharing my being gay with him? After the wedding, I went back to Vancouver, but things had changed, or maybe it was me?

After a very long three months and no response from my mother, I went to the Gay Community Center library and found a book by Betty Friedan, President of PFLAG (Parents Friends Lesbians and Gays), entitled *Now That You Know*. Vancouver's only queer-friendly bookstore, Little Sisters, had a copy and mailed it to my parents. My mother later told me she had kept everything to herself for those months, not quite knowing how she would break the news to my dad. She said it was the only secret that she had kept from him in their 35 years of marriage. That book broke the ice for them, and they would read it together in bed just before going to sleep. Working in the community library certainly had paid off in ways I could never have expected.

During the long anxious wait to hear back from my mother, things started to change for me yet again. My Wreck Beach friends from the summer were pursuing other interests as it was now approaching Vancouver's wet season, and I found myself alone a lot of the time. Not knowing why I began to stay inside reading almost every queer-themed fiction and nonfiction I could borrow from the library. I started to slip back into yet another form of a closet. One that was darker and more isolated.

My family doctor suggested a professional counsellor and recommended a gay psychiatrist who might be able to help. My opinion of psychiatrists was not high, and I certainly didn't consider myself as having a mental illness, but back in the mid-80s if you wanted help to accept yourself as being gay, you had to sign yourself over to professional help. I soon found myself in a group of 8 men, along with a clinical psychologist and my psychiatrist, doing group therapy. The program was held at St. Paul's Hospital and for 15 weeks we would meet for a couple of hours to express and confess.

For me, it was a way to cure my negative thoughts about being gay and move on. But for many others, it was a place to share their pain and abuse that they had suffered throughout their lives. The only rule was that there could be no emotional or physical attachments during the program period. That lasted about six weeks for me, and I fell for one of my fellow attendees. After we had broken the rule the first time, we knew we had to confess at the next session. As luck would have it, someone else had a week so bad they needed to take up the entire session.

With no time to confess our transgression of the group therapy rules we continued on seeing each other and decided we had come this far we're not going to stop now. What could they do? Kick us out? The next week, when it was our turn to speak, we explained what had happened and apologized to the group. But said we didn't intend to stop seeing each other outside of our weekly sessions. To our surprise, several members of the group asked what took us so long? They saw this coming a few weeks ago. What a relief it was to have acceptance from the group, and for me, that was better than all the therapy we were supposed to be receiving.

In early Spring of 1985, I joined a group of men and women who had been producing and making Gay and Lesbian content public television since 1980. I went from being the closeted gay man not wanting to be identified as queer in public, to being the co-host of a public TV program called Gayblevision.

This queer-produced program was, at the time, the only openly Gay and Lesbian TV show in North America. Great notables such as author and playwright Tennessee Williams appeared on the show along with many local and international singers, comedians, performers and authors. The show aired monthly and was produced through Rogers Cable TV in the West End. We were even invited to attend the San Francisco Gay Film Festival to pick our brains on how to produce a locally run Queer TV show. Needless to say, we were very proud to have been asked to attend such a public event.

Not satisfied to do just television I joined a local theatre company as a volunteer. When the producer became ill, I took his place and produced gay-themed theatre under the rebranded name, *Vancouver Gay Community Theatre Company*.

During this time, the Canadian Federal Government had formed a five-member, non-partisan committee that would travel across Canada seeking opinions and stories of why Canada should include sexual orientation in the Charter of Human Rights. Having access to TV camera equipment a decision was made to interview the committee members as this could help ensure the rights of the LGBTQ community. The military and police forces were definitely not in favour of inclusion, and many of my friends and acquaintances had received dishonourable discharges from the Canadian military…just because they were queer. My partner and I also took to the streets to interview complete strangers walking by. I would ask for their opinions and thoughts as to whether sexual orientation should be included in the Canadian Charter of Human Rights. The responses were overwhelmingly positive.

Since my activist years in the queer community, I have seen major growth and positive change both in acceptance from society and in protection by law. This has paved the way for Canadian LGBTQ people to be open, happy and healthy citizens. I like to think that I had a small part in helping bring that about. *When life hands you lemons, make lemon aid.*

-Claude Hewitt

Marsha Ablowitz

Marsha Ablowitz was surprised to wake up one day, ageing. She used to be a psychotherapist and climb up icy mountains. Now she researches the dark recesses of her own shrinking brain and toddles up small green hills. Marsha returns as often as possible to the Himalayas in India and the rainforest mountains of British Columbia. She explores all over the world, and she is always happy to come home.

Marsha's stories take you to high mountains, Vancouver's GLBT community and into her lively Jewish family. She studied creative writing at UBC in the 1960's, and though she had several publications, she realized writing wasn't going to put food on the table. So she worked as a social worker/therapist for over 30 years. In the 1970's she led Vancouver's first: women's self-defense groups, sexual abuse groups and the first lesbian support groups.

Now Marsha makes a lot of cedar wood chips carving masks and is happy to be writing as part of a creative GLBT group. She also writes on Hubpages and has had 8000 hits in 9 months. Visit her site: http://hubpages.com/profile/marshacanada

Photo credit: Ellen Wordsworth

My Career as a GLBT Therapist

When I first applied to be director of the West End Community Mental Health team I was refused. They gave the pitiful excuse that I needed experience and training in Mental Health. I was a bit pissed off, but I wanted a higher salary, so I applied to work on West 2 psychiatry ward at UBC Hospital. I got that job because the ward Head Psychiatrist liked the fact that I was a street social worker. I was wandering around the West End, meeting street people, hustlers, homeless youth and I was running groups with West End women, transvestites, and drug users.

After a year working as ward social worker at UBC psychiatry, I was getting a bit claustrophobic working indoors, so I applied to the newly formed Kitsilano Community Mental Health team. They hired me because I knew the jargon and had three years of post-MSW (Master of Social Work), community, youth, and mental health experience. My job was to include: hiring staff, community mental health programming, clinical supervision, and carrying a small caseload.

I had just started work, mainly as a therapist and clinical supervisor, when work started to get close to my private life. The local gay gossip line had quickly spread the word. Gays began calling to see me. I now realize the rumour wasn't that I was a brilliant psychotherapist just that I was the only out gay and my counselling was free.

Paul had heard of me through friends and the Vancouver liberation movement protests. I was surprised to see him. He was sitting in the waiting room when he looked up at me and smiled. Paul was a short, slightly built man with long reddish hair and a well-trimmed beard. He had bright blue eyes, and could easily pass as a 1950's coffeehouse beatnik in his black turtleneck and creased blue jeans.

"Hi, Paul come on in."

All I had in my office was a dark yellow shag carpet and a desk with a folding chair, so we sat on the floor because the team had just moved in and the furniture hadn't arrived yet.

The room was dark because the walls and ceiling were painted totally flat black. There was a shiny brass floor lamp in the corner. Our team had just moved in and started to work, and since some of us like the black and the shag, we kept the décor as is. I did a brief mental status assessment, and he was not having any serious mental problems. His problem was sexual.

"I'm in a relationship with George. We really love each other, and we're both in the peoples' liberation. We're attracted to each other, but I can only get an erection and ejaculate if he whips me," he said.

I had no clue about sex therapy; it wasn't mentioned in any of my courses.

"So how is that?" I said.

"Well, he doesn't want to spank me. He feels bad. Like he's the oppressor."

I could relate to George's feelings. I felt the same way... Yuck!

"Yes, I can see how he feels," I said.

"But I've always been this way since I was a kid. My dad never paid any attention to me. He never touched me or hugged me. Maybe he was gay, or maybe something else. But if I was bad, he would pull down my pants and stretch me out across his lap and spank me. He would get aroused, and I would get an erection."

"Oh, I see," I said. I still had no idea how to help, but luckily Paul ignored my confused expression and continued explaining his situation.

"So ever since then, I have fantasized that scene when I masturbate. I tried S&M with some guys who are into it, but I didn't really like them. They scared me. And I really love George we do so much political action together and we both like art and we can talk together for hours and hours."

"Yes, George seems like a really good guy," I said. I was starting to get a vague idea. I was also sometimes turned on by S&M fantasies.

"So, the problem is that George won't whip you or spank you, but when you fantasize or masturbate things really work?" I asked.

"Yes, when I fantasize everything works just fine." He replied.

"Well, how about you just fantasize that you're being whipped when you're making love with George?"

"Wouldn't that be cheating? I mean thinking about my dad when I'm making love with George?" He said.

"I don't think so. Lots of people have sexual fantasies all different kinds of sexual fantasies. Besides you don't have to tell him." I said.

"Well for sure... it's just that I really don't like being dishonest." He said.

"You could just try it out once," I said.
The next week Paul called me to cancel his appointment.
"Hey, Marsha I don't need to come again. It worked."

******

It all seemed too easy, just like that I was a gay sex therapist.
We had been running the team for a few months when the team receptionist buzzed my office and said there was a problem with a woman on the line. This woman was asking for me by my name but wouldn't give her own name. I was a bit confused and anxious.

"What is the problem?" I asked.

"She won't give me her name, and she won't tell me what it is about," said our receptionist.

"Well I guess I'd better talk to her," I said.
"Is this Marsha Ablowitz?" The woman asked. She sounded scared.

"Yes, I'm Marsha," I said.

"I need to see you. I'm thinking of killing myself."

A lot of gays killed themselves. I had to see her right away. "I'll see you today," I said.

"But I don't want my name or address in your records," She emphasized.

"Why not?"

"I'm a doctor, and I can't have my name in your system," she said.

Yikes, I thought. She's suicidal, so I need to see her quickly. But our regulations were that every client we saw had to live in our catchment area and be registered in our system. I had to do something.

"Well, how about give me some friend's address and some other name for my record," I said.

"Is that OK?" She asked.

"Why not? At least we can meet and talk and try to figure something out."

"OK, just call me Brenda Wood," She said.

"Yes, and how about coming over now?" I replied.

"Brenda" was tall, slim, with mousy brown hair tied back in a bun. She was dressed in a tailored form-fitting grey suit. Her eyes and nose were red. She entered my office quickly and sat on the new office couch. She was looking at the yellow shag rug shaking.

"Thanks for seeing me so quickly," she said.

"I'm glad you could come today."

"I just can't use my real name. It might be bad for my work as a doctor if people found out."

"That's OK," I said. "I'll just call you Brenda."
"Brenda is my aunt's name. I really like her," she said.

"Why are you feeling so terrible?" I asked. She started crying, and I passed her some Kleenex.

"I was lovers with a woman. She was my first woman lover, Linda...She was so beautiful. It was so wonderful. I only wanted her. I left my husband for her. We were going to live together," she said.

"What happened?" I asked.

"I rented a new apartment; we were furnishing it together. We got such a beautiful bed and dressers. Then just the day before she was supposed to move in with me, she left me a message from the airport. She flew back to Halifax, back to her old boyfriend."

"I'm so sorry," I said. "How are you doing?"

"I can't sleep. I can't eat. I can't go to work. I'm collecting pills to overdose."

"Do you have those pills with you?" I asked. "Yes, in my purse."

"Would you let me keep them for a while?"

"Well, I don't know."

"Just for a while. We can keep meeting and talking. I'll return them to you when you ask me."

"Will you tell anyone?"

"No. I'll lock the pills in my desk drawer."

She paused a long while looking at me. "Yes, I'll give them to you."

I put the pill bottles in a plain brown envelope and sealed it. I wrote Brenda and the date on the envelope and locked it in my drawer. I wrote her an appointment for next week.

"Come and see me next week and in the meantime call me if you feel like you might hurt yourself." "Brenda" did not call me.

The next week "Brenda" looked much better. Her eyes were clear. She was more relaxed. She smiled a little shaky smile.

"I'm back at work."

"Good, how are you feeling?"

"Miserable, but I'm OK at work."

We spoke about her plans for the future. I gave her contact information for some women's groups and some gay groups.

"I think I'm OK now. I'd like my pills back."

I unlocked my desk and handed her the brown envelope.

******

As I continued counselling gays, my self-confidence improved. I even told the staff at work to stop telling anti-gay jokes and rude terms for gays. Some people were pissed off, but it made work easier for me. Of course, the whole staff and mental service soon knew I was gay. One day as I was chatting with a colleague at the Kitsilano Mental Health Team, I first saw Jean hanging out in our waiting room. Embarrassed I looked away. "Why does she have to wear a man's shirt? How come she's got a boy's haircut?" Then, Judy, our Occupational Therapist asked:

"Marsha, can Jean join your hiking group?"

"Well, it's pretty full... but yeah, I guess so."

"She's really sweet and Marsha, it might be really good for her to talk with you."

My stomach clenched. Fuck, had Judy told this patient I was gay? Well, it was my own damn fault for being out at work. But I was out to my staff, not to my clients.

Jean was a dark slim teenager from some hick, god-forsaken town in the interior. Her parents and probably the whole town had kicked her out. She ended up in Vancouver, in the hospital and was discharged to our mental health team with a vague diagnosis of manic depression and some sort of sexual identity disorder. She seemed pretty sane to me.

Driving to the hike, I avoided Jean. I put her in the back seat with two other clients. Jean bounced in the back seat laughing and joking around with the guys. When we parked in the UBC forest, I hiked on ahead. She ran to catch up with me as we descended the path.

"Marsha-I heard that gays are legal in Holland."

"Um, yes I've heard they are legal there."

"Do you think it will ever be legal in Canada?'

"Um...I don't know."

"And I heard that gays are even allowed to get married in Holland."

"Yes, they are."

"Do you think it might happen here?"

"Maybe, some day. Maybe you could go to Holland."
I sure wasn't all that helpful.

Judy asked me how Jean did on the hike I said "Fine." Actually, I was starting to really like Jean. She was smart, lively with dark eyes and a quick smile. When I'd see her around the mental health team, I'd always say "Hi."

Then one morning at the staff meeting Judy was frantic, "Jean missed her appointment yesterday. She never misses her appointments. She's never even late."
"Maybe she's left town."

"I went over to her rooming house. Her landlady was worried. Jean just disappeared. Everything in her room is totally neat. All her stuff is still there."
A few days later a police officer called Judy. Jean's body had been found in the bushes under the south end of the Burrard Bridge. Judy's appointment card was in Jean's pocket. After meeting with the cops, Judy was crying.

"Marsha the police say Jean jumped off the bridge. How can they just decide that? Jean wasn't depressed or suicidal. She didn't leave a note. She was so happy when I talked with her last time. She'd just met a nice girl."

"What do you think happened?'

"She used to walk home from that gay club downtown. She couldn't afford bus fare so she'd walk down

Burrard and across the bridge. I told her it wasn't safe. Guys were hanging out on the street outside at closing time. They kept following her and threatening her. The police don't even want to investigate."

"Um… O.K., Judy, I'll talk to the police."

The police officer agreed that he would find time to come over to our office. He was a gigantic guy standing very straight in his crisp blue uniform, looming over me. He had all the accessories: silvery badge, wide belt, shiny leather holster, gun.

"Officer, why aren't you going to investigate Jean's death?" I asked.

"No need to waste our time. We know what happened."

"How can you know without investigating?"

"We're experienced. We know what we are doing."

"But officer she wasn't depressed. Men were following her. She might have been attacked."

"No, we know she jumped. She had a reason. We have evidence."
He smirked down at me. My throat was dry. I looked down.

Finally, I said, "What reason, what evidence?"

"They do it, those people."

"What?" I couldn't speak.

He shifted, hummed and hawed, sort of chuckled and cleared his throat. "Well we know she was...you know...she was one of those... homos... You know, she was a "boy-girl."

-Marsha Ablowitz

Michael Yoder

Michael has lived in British Columbia since 1969. He emerged from his closet in 1979 and took the doors off after that. In his late teens and early 20s, he was involved in helping to organize social gatherings for gay men. Michael studied music composition at the University of Victoria and after that became involved in community advocacy. After being diagnosed with HIV in 1995, Michael joined the board of directors of the Victoria Persons Living with HIV/AIDS Society (now the Vancouver Island Persons Living with HIV/AIDS Society - VPWAS). He worked as Executive Director of the Victoria AIDS Resource & Community Service Society (VARCS) until 1996. He served on the Canadian AIDS Society board of directors from 1998 - 2003. Michael currently is a Peer Navigator and facilitator of "POZitively Connected" with VPWAS.

Photo credit: Ron Kearse

There's No Place Like Home

When I was a boy, every Easter we would watch The Wizard of Oz on TV, eating popcorn and drinking Orange Crush. I was always mesmerized once Dorothy ended up in the technicolour world of Munchkin Land and the story had me captivated. At the end of the movie, I would always cry: I didn't want Dorothy to go back to that sepia-tinted world where everything seemed so unhappy, leaving a world full of strange magical characters that cared about her.

I was born in California, and we moved to Victoria in 1969 when I was eight years old. My father had passed from cancer, and my mother didn't get along with her in-laws. Her parents lived in Victoria, and so we left: I was completely distraught leaving everything I knew for this place that we learned in school was our *Great White Neighbour to the North*. I was certain there were no cars or television, everyone lived in igloos, and it snowed all year long. That's what American kids learn about Canada.

Being eight years old in a new place, new country, new house with no friends was not easy. I had no conception of *gay* at that age; I was just me. I liked playing with the few kids on the block and going to the beach at the end of the street, building rafts and floating into Gonzales Bay with little more than sticks to propel us.

But school was where terror started. The teachers liked me. My Grade three teacher was a kind woman who welcomed me into the class halfway through the year. I was a bright kid and did well, but she pointed that out to the whole class, and my life ended. I could feel the lump in my stomach knowing that the bullying would get worse: I was the teacher's pet. Soon, the other boys were calling me *fag* and *fem* boy, words I didn't understand and a loathing I didn't understand, other than whatever they were calling me was "bad," and they were equating me with the girls. The words were so painful and deeply wounding that I knew I couldn't tell my mother. She might think the same terrible things about me.

In the 1970s there was no *gay* on TV, there was no RuPaul's Drag Race or Graham Norton. I had no frame of reference for who I was. I was only a kid, and as a kid, I didn't even know how babies got made, let alone anything *gay*. But whatever I was, I didn't fit; I didn't belong. I was alone in a world that couldn't accept me.

Where I found support, was with teachers. I liked learning, and I liked the encouragement they offered me. My grandmother and mother were also supportive. I was an *artsy kid,* and they gave me space to be who I was through my creativity.

My grandmother especially was my friend. Every Sunday I would bike over to my grandparents' house where the smell of freshly baked bread would fill the place. We'd have lunch and talk and listen to the radio. In the afternoon, she would teach me things like oil painting and crafts, or I would just watch her as she indulged in her own creativity. In a desert with no friends, her house was an oasis for me.

In Grade 6, my teacher got me interested in speech classes and theatre. I liked being in school pageants and plays and she coached me into entering the local poetry competitions. At her house, we would talk, and I would practice my speeches. She was always a gentle soul and a taskmaster too, but I appreciated that guidance. She knew I didn't fit and in a way, she didn't fit either. As a teacher, she was tough; the other kids didn't like her. Perhaps she felt some connection with me; we were both misfits. And she accepted me for who I was and encouraged me to express my creativity.

Leaving elementary school and entering junior high was like rearranging deck chairs on the Titanic. All the bullies from Grade three followed me, and there were new ones, too.

My mother finally got me to tell her about the bullying, but I never told her why they were bullying me. I couldn't. There were no words for me yet about being gay, even though I knew I was *different*. The school counsellor made me tell him the names of some of the kids, but I begged him not to say anything.

That was stupid. He called them in, and then my life got even worse. School was so terrible for me that I would get physically ill at the thought of going there. I would do anything I could to avoid going to school and eventually had to take a lot of grade eight by correspondence.

There were safe spaces for me and again, it was all about art and theatre. I loved being able to be me in art class, and I loved my teachers for it. They encouraged individuality and expression, and most of us in those classes were outsiders, the ones who didn't *fit*.

My Grade eight drama teacher was pivotal for me in understanding my identity, whatever that was, (I still had no real idea about sex and sexual orientation). And the experience of knowing him also confirmed my fears about being *different*. He was a great teacher: he loved to play and stretch our imaginations. I was in heaven! And there was something about him that said to me *I'm like him*, but I wasn't certain what that meant.

Partway through the year, he wasn't at school anymore. There were rumours about why he left, but I don't really know why. I never saw him again, and I was saddened. The one man who was like me was gone because he was *different* like me. The closet doors were shut even tighter. I still wonder what happened to him and where he is now. The safe space was gone.

Then there was a time in homeroom where the other boys were talking about masturbating: a word I think they read in the dictionary. They said "Hey, Yoder! I bet YOU don't masturbate!" Since they were clearly doing it, I replied "Yeah! Of course, I do!"

Then I had to find the school dictionary where masturbation was described as *sexual self-abuse*. Well, I didn't do that! But in fact, I'd been masturbating for some time to a greater or lesser extent, and the images in my head were always men. I'd seen a few men naked and was fascinated by their penises because they seemed too big and they had hair.

Then came the sex talk with my mother. She tried as best she could to let me know how babies were made and I remember at the end that she said, "if you choose to go with boys, that's okay too. As long as you're happy." And I thought, *but, how do I make babies with a boy?*

High school and the bullying didn't end, only this time there were girl bullies as well. Boy bullies are much more up front - they hit you, call you names, chase you...but girl bullies are different. Looking for emotional buttons, their abuse is more mental than physical, and the scars are even deeper. Again, I found safe spaces in art and theatre, the places where it was okay being *different*. By Grade eleven there were a few of us who were gay together. I'd realized that I was attracted to guys and knew more about what that meant. The few of us were comfortable being together - we could be ourselves without fear.

My teachers were also a source of safety. They loved it when creative kids did creative things and lapped up the information they were sharing. At the same time, I was entering that *rebellious* phase of skipping classes and hanging out with friends. Sex didn't enter into it, and I still wasn't sure about what it all meant for me. At one point, I fell madly in love with a boy who was also in theatre. We could finish each other's sentences and would take long walks at night, talking and joking and going for coffee. He wasn't gay, but every moment with him was heaven for me.

Then one night, when I needed to escape my family, I stumbled on the local cruising area. There was a man who kept walking past me, and I wondered why. The lightbulb went off, and I knew this was my chance to have sex. We drove around in his car and finally found a dark, quiet side street. The sex was basic: oral and jerking off and afterward when he drove me home, I thought *is that it?* But I was now a *man*, no longer the virgin youth I was engaged in gay sex, and I liked it, a lot!

I started spending more and more time at the cruising spot and met other gay men. I had sex with some of them, but a lot of the time it was just talking or going for a late coffee. At seventeen, being with these men and having adult conversations and learning innuendo - which can be subtle enough to go over my head, was a part of my learning curve about being gay.

Then I met my first boyfriend. Apparently, he had money. I didn't think about that, but there were other young guys who liked him because he could buy them things. He drove a Firebird, which should have triggered me to understand that he had money, but I just liked being with him - and the sex was fantastic.

We would go to movies together and surreptitiously hold hands in the dark theatre. We would go for food and play footsies under the table, and we would make passionate sex. I'd rented my first little bachelor suite, and the freedom to be sexual in my own place was something I had longed for.

Then one evening he took me to the local gay club. It was 1979, and the anthem was *I Will Survive* by Gloria Gaynor. It was the height of the disco era, and gay clubs were popular, mostly in larger cities, but the fact that we had even *one* was amazing for a small, conservative government town.

Dorothy was swept up in a tornado, the house swirling and pitching in the wind. Images of the witch and cows and neighbours were twisting past her in the sepia world.

When we got to the Queens Head, I was terrified. Underage and having never been to any club before, I wondered what it would be like. We got to the door and I remember my heart was racing.

The house landed with a thud. Dorothy got off the bed and made her way to the door. She opened it. Before her was a world full of colour and strange sights - bold bright flowers and gardens and a yellow swirl of bricks alongside a swirl of red.

Inside the club, the music was pounding. Loud disco played the latest dance hits - the Bee Gees, Gloria Gaynor, the Hustle, now so old, but then so fresh and full of life. A disco ball and coloured lights swirled around the room. We ordered drinks and sat down. I tried to take it all in: men were dancing together, and women were dancing together, and there was kissing and hand holding, and I felt a rush. This was not the straight world that rejected me. This was not a place where bullies were going to harm me. I had finally landed out of the tornado in which I grew up, and the house that dropped landed squarely on the Wicked Witch that had tormented me for so many years. This was a place where I could be me - gay and open and *out!*

This was home.

-Michael Yoder

Pat Hogan

Pat Hogan was born and raised in a small New England mill town. She's lived in New York City, Santa Barbara and San Francisco California before moving to Canada in 1969, and maintains dual citizenship in the US & Canada.

Pat is an Organizer, Writer, Activist, Creator/Initiator of Events/Organizations, Feminist, Lesbian, Dancer, Communicator, Witch and Communitarian. She has many years of Office/Administrative experience and Court Reporter Training. Over the years she has taken college courses and has no degrees.

She is a proud mother of a son and daughter plus five grandchildren.

Photo credit: Karen Lamica

Blame it on the Wimmin!

It was that damn feminism that did it! I'm sure of it. If I hadn't gone to the Okanagan on my way to, I don't know where, with two kids in tow, escaping a violent hetero relationship, I might not be the hardcore dyke I am today. I'd still be a hippy chick! Well come to think of it, I am that too!

But seriously, that's the way it happened. Living out of a van, finding a home, enrolling the kids in school, finding the women's centre and forging onward; the rest unfolded, in time.

I wasn't totally in the dark about feminism. I was involved with alternative and feminist actions and activities in Vancouver prior to arriving in the Okanagan– collective daycares, food buying collectives, collective households, and so on – but THIS was different.

It was the mid 70's, the Decade of Women was in full gear, and the Vernon Women's Centre was lobbying their MLA for abortion rights, equal pay for women and many other rights. The BC Federation of Women, more familiarly known as the BCFW was a radical (for that time) action-oriented feminist group, a de-centralized, province-wide organization composed of women's groups throughout BC who met regularly, rotating meetings from one end of the province to the other, billeting women, providing childcare. Securing government grant money while modest, helped with room rentals, childcare and transportation. We stretched those dollars and created an amazingly firm feminist foundation. The time was ripe to start a revolution. We wanted change, and we wanted it NOW!

I have fond memories of hitchhiking from the Okanagan to Vancouver, Nelson and other places for meetings. Those were the days!

When I got there, I decided that the Okanagan was as good as any place to be. Nelson, which I had considered moving to was a hotbed of women's groups, and so I learned later, a hotbed of lesbians! But it was too far. I had been on the road long enough.

I arrived just in time for BCFW's annual meeting, hosted by the Women's Centre. It didn't take long. Suddenly I was the North Okanagan rep to the BCFW. I was excited about being one of them, strategizing and organizing to make positive changes in women's lives. I was in awe of the fervour and passion that I witnessed in these women.

"Hey, Pat, can you take care of organizing billets for the women who won't be staying at the Vernon Lodge?" I was asked my first week volunteering at the centre. "Oh sure," I said confidently, not knowing a soul in Vernon, but what the hell, I'd figure it out. Thanks to supportive women and my fly-by-the-seat-of-my-pants attitude I managed to pull it off. I was on my way to organizing!

While the Vernon women's centre was a drop-in place for all women, many of whom were hippy rural women who lived outside of Vernon, the centre was started, and very much run, by local women. Totally committed to feminist principles, most held prominent positions in town, or their husbands did -- teachers, doctors, lawyers etc. There was an unspoken difference between mainstream feminists and women who lived alternative lifestyles. And then, there were the lesbians!

At our first BCFW meeting at the AGM, after introductions, a woman stood up and in a strident, forceful voice, announced, "We need a lesbian caucus in BCFW." *A lesbian caucus?? Why? I naively wondered. Aren't we all working for the same things?* One thing about the BCFW: the members were much more left of centre than the women who ran the women's centre, both in appearance and in their politics.

I looked around the room packed with women, mostly in the 30 to 50-age range, Birkenstocks, jeans, long hair, short hair, all sizes.

Then I saw two women kissing. *Oh my God! Lesbians! How do I act in front of them? Will they think I'm uncool because I'm straight?* Even then, I felt like they had a secret club and I wanted to know more, but afraid I'd be the outsider.

It's not that I didn't know lesbians. Many of us recent ex-US Pats, and Canadians alike were back to the land types and hung out together. The lesbian land communities and hippy communes often existed side by side. Many women started out in hetero or mixed communes and as they came out, gradually formed their own lesbian communes and communal houses.

Hippies and dykes, we lived in our respective communities, moving out of urban centres to BC's interior, finding other like-minded people, broken down cabins and fixing them up.

We were also sneaking draft dodgers and their families across the border in the middle of the night to find a new life in Canada.

Some of the dykes lived in Vancouver, their small apartments a refuge for the herds hitching in and out of Vancouver on a weekly basis, a motley gang of long-haired women, and men, long skirts, no underwear, women with women - dykes and straights and kids. We made our way down to Famous Foods on East Hastings to pick up our 50# bag of brown rice (au natural, of course!), another 50# bag of oatmeal, Soy sauce, odds and ends and a stop at the Anchor Inn for a beer.

"Hey Pat, we're going down to the Vanport tonight. Want to come?" I was asked on one of these trips into town. Want to come? I didn't even know what the Vanport was, but if the women were going, so was I. New country, new friends, new lifestyle! There was much to learn.

The Vanport was a notorious and grungy bar on Main Street near Chinatown, usually with a mix of sailors fresh off the ship looking to pick up women, and the dykes. Many a fight broke out when a guy tried to pick up a dyke. The guys didn't have a fighting chance with some pretty tough women knocking the wind out of them.

All this was before I moved to the Okanagan. My life changed radically with that move.

The lesbians in the BCFW were activists and fighters. They were at every march, every rally, speaking out for ALL women, and children. But, where were their straight sisters when it came to lesbian issues? They weren't there. I finally got why there was a need for a lesbian caucus. They needed to discuss, vent, strategize and make proposals to the larger feminist community in order to be included, respected, listened to. They needed to fight, with other feminists, for their sexuality choices and lifestyles.

The lesbian caucuses created a division with some of the straight feminists. They were being challenged to move from their comfort zone and into foreign territory! "Lesbian" was not a comfortable word nor was it comfortable being around lesbians when they talked their lesbian talk, showed affection toward their partner or flirted with a straight woman!

Straight feminists were having to examine their own phobias. It wasn't easy and didn't happen quickly, but in time the entire women's movement started to change. They had to take a look at their structure – mostly white middle-class women - their values, and their resistance to change.

The movement at that time was a white women's movement – i.e. feminism and lesbianism --the movement that was most obvious and in the public eye at any rate. All that changed when racism started to be addressed in the feminist community. But that was later.

Young women today who use *"feminist"* to describe themselves whether they identify as *queer, lesbian, bi, trans or straight,* are a different breed. They've inherited the herstory of these struggles and their freedom to be who they want to be.

During this period of my life, (and to this day) I was wrapped up in women – at work, socially, politically. There were few men in my life.

It was only a matter of time when I would come out. In fact, it took me a couple of years to come out, to myself, to my grown kids – who were not happy about my life. They just wanted me to be *"normal."*

Having casual sex with women, but calling it *"just flings"* (not a relationship) was the slow process of me finally saying out loud to myself: *"I'm a lesbian."* It was scary. I was in my mid-40's. Would I lose friends, family, kids? It wasn't an easy time, I had self-doubts about where I was headed, but I knew it was where I was supposed to be.

My first real big love, Barb, was a dyke from Ontario whom I met when she took a trip in her truck to the west coast to heal from a breakup of a long-term relationship. She was a lesbian separatist, and I was once again, learning about the dyke community. I learned quickly. She had travelled with a band of lesbians across the US, Mexico and Canada, on the search for lesbian land, lesbian communities, all that was woman. As much as possible, they avoided having to do anything with men, including where they shopped etc. There were lots of women at the time moving into the trades, challenging the male status quo regarding jobs, training and more. Good timing, indeed.

Then there was the lesbian separatist/image thing. First: I didn't walk with large enough steps, I needed more black clothing, to wear leather, and so on. I was being reshaped, trained to be a REAL dyke. I never did really make the grade, but I tried! Barb could be loving, fun and she could be fierce. She scared me at times. I was trying so hard to fit in.

The thing is, she loved, simply loved, dyke life. She was the original Dyke on the Road with her ex-lover and a whole gang of rebel, break-all-rules wimmin, seeking lesbian nirvana. Shaven heads, beards for some, no male anything, including her dogs. Don't ever call them *"he"*. She'd go ballistic. Yet, like most lesbian separatists, there were contradictions. Even though they aspired to no contact with the patriarchy, including all men, they still had fathers and brothers and bought food and gas in the patriarchal world. Interestingly, Barb and my son liked each other. However, when she lived in a communal dyke household in Vancouver, a never to be broken house rule was that there were no men in the house, ever. These were hard times for me. I was enthralled with her life, with her, and yet I had a son whom I loved, a teenager who had been moved around, separated from his father (for a good reason). I tried hard to let him know he was loved and accepted.

In time Barb and I drifted apart and then together again and then apart. During one of the apart times, Barb was diagnosed with cancer. I re-connected with her, and although she moved back to Ontario, I was there when she died.

Thanks to Barb, I met lots of lesbians and was firmly entrenched in the community. Since those early days of lesbian feminism, I continue to create, organize and build community organizations like:

• An East-Side Vancouver community Café, *(Josephine's)* which became a place for dykes to hang out, a venue for social and political events and where women's art & crafts were sold. A monthly meeting place for trans folks.
• A production company, *Sounds & Furies*, which still brings in some of the most revered lesbian performers from across Canada and the US as well as organizing social, political and spiritual workshops and events
• A same-sex Ballroom Dance group, *Not So Strictly Ballroom*, which teaches ballroom, Argentine Tango and other dances. Several NSSB members competed in Gay Games Dance competitions around the world.
• *BC Witchcamp*, which celebrates its 30th year in 2018. A weeklong training, based on the teachings

and work of Reclaiming, a San Francisco political and spiritual group, whose co-founder, Starhawk, is known globally for her writings, films, activism, drumming and rituals.

• Founder and co-organizer of BOLDFest, an annual Conference and Gathering for bold, old (er) Lesbians & Dykes, attended by 150+ women from across Canada and the US and internationally, ranging in age from 30's to 80's+

-Pat Hogan

Val Innes

Val is a transplanted Scot, to Winnipeg in 1958 and then the West Coast in 1991. A retired university instructor with Masters degrees in English and Education, a feminist, a writer, an artist, a builder who loves winter holidays in Mexico and summer holidays at an Ontario lake, Val cannot picture a life without politics, without an effort to make the world a better, more equal place, any more than she can picture it without books, writing, women or deep, intense talk. She has lived with that politicization as a background, teaching and volunteering in various organizations, as well as marching and protesting to help bring about positive change.

Photo credit: Val Innes

Transition -- Beyond Silence

Looking back over my life from the vantage point of seventy-one years, I think my story is probably not an uncommon one. Born in 1946 in Scotland into a middle-class, white family with all the privileges that brings with it, I didn't fit the norm. That didn't become evident until the 60s and 70s, when, like many others of my generation, I rebelled at the culture I lived in. And not just because I became a lesbian, although *because* of that, my life changed and I became political, stronger and clearer about who I was and what I wanted to do.

My mother wanted a girl who would wear dresses with grace, who would play with dolls and who would, ultimately marry and provide her with grandchildren. I wasn't that girl. Far more comfortable with bikes, tennis racquets, cricket bats, model aeroplanes and cars, I cut my hair to rid myself of the curlers she would put me in at night. The nearby train track, my friend's oversize bike, my brother's cars and a nearby park were far more of a draw than anything femininity could provide.

I was incapable of wearing the face and clothes demanded of a North American woman in the 70s. I could not stand the weight of nail polish and the lie of makeup. I had no interest in dresses, nylons, high heels and all the trappings; I wanted jeans and T-shirts and physical freedom.

After I came out, I never wore a dress again.

My dad, though, didn't care whether I looked feminine or not; he wanted me happy, busy and successful in school, and I was. He was the one who took us to Canada. We immigrated to Winnipeg, Manitoba in December 1958, via London, the Queen Mary, New York and Toronto. I loved the sea voyage, but I still had no idea about where I was going, or that when I said goodbye to my best friend, at the train station in Aberdeen, I would never see her again.

Then we arrived in Winnipeg to snow drifts higher than my head and thirty below zero temperatures. As an immigrant, for the first time in my life, I really experienced being an outsider, an exile. Immigrating to Canada meant becoming *the other*, in no uncertain terms, in a strange, vast, country, full of straight streets and painted wood houses. Scotland, my extended family, school and my culture, were far away. I spoke differently and behaved differently from the people in this new world. Nothing and no one that was familiar or loved by me was important to the people here.

I still had my family though, small as it was. It was a happy family, but there were secrets and silences in it, too. Some I never understood for years after, long after my child's voice had become adult. We never talked about what made us angry or unhappy; that was not acceptable.

Then my mother became ill and almost died when I was sixteen, something that shaped the rest of my life. When she was recovering, my father said to me, "if you're upset at your mother, don't tell her; don't get angry. You might kill her," That silenced me even more. I only became aware, as an adult, much later, of what an impact that had on my life.

She survived but was a semi-invalid for the rest of her life – sixteen more years, threaded with operations and scares, ambulances screeching towards hospitals and survival yet again after much breath-taking waiting. And life went on. I completed high school, dated, went to university, and became part of a really great group of people. I thought I was in love with Paul, a lovely boy-man, but wouldn't wear his fraternity pin or consider marrying him and waved him off to Africa and CUSO. I finished a degree in English, travelled in Europe with a close friend, returned to complete a Master's and went into education.

I was, quite thoroughly, a product of the sixties. Like Dylan, I was convinced that "the times they are a'changin" (Dylan, 1964) – and they were. During my high school and undergraduate years, John F Kennedy had promised Camelot and was assassinated; Martin Luther King had dreamed of a better world and was assassinated. Robert Kennedy had started his run for president on the same theme and was assassinated, and few in my circle believed that these deaths were coincidental. The civil rights movement still flourished, though, with race riots in major cities; the civil rights bill got signed into law in the States by Lyndon Baines Johnson, and people my age from Canada, were down south helping to register black voters; some never came back.

The cold war was constantly in the background when it was not in the foreground (Bay of Pigs); the Berlin Wall went up; the Vietnam War proceeded. Kent State taught us that the police could not be trusted. In Canada, Diefenbaker gave Status Indians the vote in 1960. Pearson recognized Quebec's status as a nation within a nation, and in 1968 Trudeaumania hit Canada. Trudeau invoked Martial Law over FLQ terrorism in Quebec and also took the state out of the bedroom, legalizing male homosexuality. Canada refused to become involved in the Vietnam War and became a destination for draft dodgers from the States.

It was a turbulent time, and I was a product of that particular, historical moment. I may not have been consciously aware of it then, but, in retrospect, it is clear that I was becoming politically critical of the society within which I lived. And then I fell in love with a woman, one of my best friends and not living in Winnipeg anymore. She was visiting, and we spent a lot of time together, as friends do. Very suddenly, it seemed at the time, I changed; one evening, I so badly wanted to kiss her, I couldn't think of much else, and later, after I told her what I was feeling, she kissed me, and I knew this was completely different than anything I had ever felt before.

That changed *my* life, but not hers, and I disappeared into a several years long attempt to become straight -- or not have a personal life. Four years later, at the end of a failed, closeted relationship and suicidal, I told my Dad. Still scared of upsetting and killing my mother, I phoned from Sharon's and asked him to come over to my place, saying I had something to tell him.

When he arrived, I looked over at my father, this man I loved and could lose. I was shaking. It took all my nerve to say anything at all. Without thinking anymore, I blurted out,

"I'm scared to say this, but I really have to tell you. I've been . . . I've been in love with Kate for years, Dad. And then I've been with another woman. I think I'm gay, Dad. I'm so unhappy; I think it'd be easier if I just died. I'm so scared you and Mum won't love me anymore." The words tumbled out once I started.

Dad's face whitened; he sighed and got up, came over and pulled me to my feet in a huge hug. "Val, you're my daughter, and I love you, no matter what happens. Nothing can change that. Your mum will feel the same. We'll help." My mother echoed this later that day, saying, "you're our daughter, and we love you, just as you are."

I hadn't lost them; I'd told the truth, and I hadn't lost them.

So, I came out to my family and friends in 1977, eleven months before my mother died. Both my parents were supportive; however, I knew both were worried. My coming out changed my family; finally, we talked about how we felt. Those were the most honest eleven months I had with my mother and father. The biggest secret I had was out now, and I didn't have to hide. My mum saw me off to my first gay dance. She saw me join Heather Bishop's guitar group and met all the women in it. She adopted the two lesbians who came to live in my house as roommates, one of them disowned by her parents when she told them she was gay.

But it wasn't all as simple as that. I was not what my family had wanted. They saw me becoming more political, more radical, more vocal, and my mum in particular, although she was very supportive and loving in many ways, tried to silence me once more, to get me to simply settle for a cottage for two with a picket fence – this time with a woman instead of a man, but the same scenario; I was supposed to "think of my family name" and hide.

I would not be silenced this time though. I was stronger, and I had support. I marched in lesbian marches in Saskatoon and Manitoba, joined a rape crisis centre as a volunteer counsellor, spoke publically and often about rape and shared my house with other lesbians. barely allowing my job to interfere with my suddenly blooming social and political life, compartmentalizing both, given the sobering reality that I now belonged to a disadvantaged minority, rather than the privileged class in which I had been born and raised, and whose protection I could no longer take for granted.

Before this I hadn't even realized I was privileged – white, middle class, educated – and others were not. As a lesbian and a budding feminist, I was now just starting to see my world from the perspective of *the other* rather than an insider. I was an exile again, an immigrant in a heterosexual world, and one who didn't want to fit in this time. My silence had been broken, and I wasn't about to go underground ever again.

I've spent the rest of my life as a lesbian – in a world I did want to fit into, as well as the heterosexual world in which I lived and taught. I've loved and lived with five women over the years; two of them are still among my best friends, all four were completely accepted by my family. I've helped organize lesbian conferences; I've been political and vocal. I've worked on social justice issues, feminist, left issues, most of my adult life. I could not, still cannot, picture my life without politics, without an effort to make the world a better, more equal place, any more than I can picture it without books, without writing, without women or without talk, deep intense, intimate talk.

I have lived my life, both personally and professionally with that politicization as a background, teaching critical thought, empowering students, many of them marginalized in one way or another, working in alternative situations and volunteering in various organizations, as well as protesting and marching, to bring about a better world. I've taught in schools, alternative, indigenous and regular, college and university, and I've always been out to my colleagues, but never fully to my students, something I have regretted. How I managed that, along with openly helping organize things like the first annual lesbian conferences in Winnipeg and Vancouver, is a bit of a mystery, but I did.

My father remarried four years after my mother died, and they had a boy, another brother for me, David – one who physically defended a young, maybe gay, kid in elementary school, saying, more or less, that his sister was gay.

Both my parents are dead now, and my family is small and blended, but they love me as I am. Neither my brother nor I had children, but I have a community of friends, here and in Winnipeg, straight and gay; some of those friends are family, too. And in my early seventies, I'm retired from teaching, but help coordinate Quirk-e, the Queer Imaging and Riting Kollective for Elders, which has just published *Basically Queer, An Intergenerational Introduction to LGBTQA2S+ Lives*. I live in White Rock instead of Winnipeg. I did the coursework for a Ph.D. on memoir, gays, lesbians and social justice -- something, along with gay marriage, that I would never have thought possible when I was coming out in the late seventies. I spent the last years of my career getting Kwantlen Faculty Association to have a LGBTQ+ representative, and I was the first LGBTQ rep in its history.

And why would I want to do this? Because I spent so many years closeted, and I compartmentalized my life into school and the rest of a completely *out* life. Complicit. Compliant, with good reason most of the time – after all, I lost a university teaching job once because I was a lesbian.

But the reasons have been internal as well as external, and it's easier now to break the silence and be who I am.

And if I can do anything to make it easier for other LGBT teachers and students to be who they are, safely, in the world, in their classrooms, that will be a worthwhile thing to do – and it will be a cleansing for me. Becoming a lesbian meant I had to be stronger, had to be engaged, had to stop being complicit. And I did.

-Val Innes

Harris Taylor

Harris Taylor is a writer, documentary filmmaker and television producer who has contributed programming to Northern Native Broadcasting, Yukon, CBC North and Vision TV since 1991. Having lived and worked in remote locations in Northern BC, Yukon, NWT and Nunavut, she developed a deep and abiding respect for the land and Canada's First Peoples. Much of her work has focused on the Aboriginal people, cultures and history across Canada's North, Disability Issues and Queer life experience. In her travels, she always takes note of the fishing spots that will someday, lure her back for another adventure.

Photo credit: Michael O'Shaughnessy
B&W image processing: Cyndia Cole

Red Boot Laces - Grise Fiord

The Tone was established on Day One at CBC Eastern Arctic when the manager gave me a tour of Iqaluit. Alone in the CBC Jeep, he said, "I objected to you being hired as Show Producer as there is a local candidate who I preferred over you."

We proceeded on Ring Road while the tour continued, "This is the Sewage Lagoon, this is the Road to Nowhere, this is the Dump..."

And that was just the beginning.

———

I stomped out of the Grise Fiord Hotel in a rage, my red boot laces slapping the dirt. I just spent two weeks with my cameraman and Inuit male reporter shooting a documentary about Quttinirpaaq National Park on top of Ellesmere Island. In Inuktitut, Quttinirpaaq means "top of the world."

It felt like the top of the world in Tanquary Fiord when my tent was battered by a blizzard on July 14. The wind was cold, but the climate of my male co-workers was *freezing*. They did not like being directed by a woman, a lesbian. They spoke to each other like I was invisible, laughed at jokes that I was not privy to.

After the storm, I unzipped my tent. An Arctic Hare chewed on the grass at my feet, unafraid as it had not yet met humans. Our camp was surrounded by wildlife. A band of Perry Caribou wandered the hills behind us in search of Lichen. Muskoxen brushed against Arctic Willow to shed last winter's ultra-warm undercoat nearby. A Polar Bear swam in the fiord and dove for a Ringed Seal. Two Arctic Wolves scouted the perimeter of our camp, looking for a quick bite.

After breakfast, the cameraman, reporter and I, packed the gear down to the beach where a helicopter would collect and deliver us to the deck of the Kapitan Khelebnikov Icebreaker. Eco-Tourism was big news, an adventure only for the very rich.

Camera rolling, we levitated over Gull Glacier, the ice hand reaching down to the Fiord. Then, out to sea for a long shot of the ship and the chop on the water as we approached her. Adventure-seeking tourists gathered on deck to watch us land. I checked the shots off my list and stored it in my pack.

Once on deck, our first stop was the Bridge, where the captain stood in control of his ship. I told the cameraman to get a medium shot of the captain, a wide shot of the captain's point-of-view out the bow window, close-ups of the captain's hands on the controls and the navigation system. It was a tight space to be in with three men.

I thanked the captain, and we toured the ship with the camera, collecting sound bites from tourists – triumphant to have conquered the North-West Passage first hand. Then, out on the deck for the reporter to do his stand up in Inuktitut.

Our flight out of Tanquary was more turbulent than our flight in. The bumps were augmented by the fact that we were exhausted and sick of each other's company.

The Tundra Tires of our Twin Otter ground to a stop on the airstrip gravel. We were back to crash for the night and rest for our flight home tomorrow. The men were distant, content to play cards with each other, eat bleeding steaks, frozen veg, instant potatoes and watch porn before loping to their lairs for the night.

A thick fog had rolled in overnight. There would be no plane out that day, the next day, or the next. Three days became three weeks. Suffocating, I was trapped with two men who were hungry to satisfy themselves by establishing power. Their daily dose of porn affirmed their right to demean and debase women. The *fuck you* attitude was underscored as a tacit threat that they could do anything that they wanted to me and get away with it.

When the fog lifted a bit, I had a chance to escape the testosterone, and I took it. Walking in town, I saw the skinny bitches with their hungry pups. The small ones enticed as they tugged the sleeves of Inuit children. Pups squealed and yipped as kids laughed and pulled away or wrapped their arms round a pup's belly and carried it off. This game of dominance was stamped into both species. They would depend on each other for life.

Outside town, I enjoyed fresh air and sea wind in my hair. Ice growled and heaved under the quick shadow of an Arctic Tern. I heard the Tern whistle as stones struck stones with each step. Careful steps knowing that if I were injured, I'd be at the mercy of the elements till found. *If found*. What a trip! Breathe this moment, remember it forever!

WOOF woke me - almost too late. I was surrounded by a pack of sled dogs, testing their chains. Blue eyes watched my blue eyes. These dogs were not playful. They were ravenous males, mean from confinement, hunger, the sting of the Musher's whip and wounds that they inflicted on each other as pack dominance was established. DANGER! Every year, sled dogs killed someone. They would smell my fear like bacon frying.

WOOF! The Alpha's low, warning bark.

I **WOOFED** back at him and stood my ground. I grew up with dogs and knew how to handle them.

Dogs sniffed the air and licked their chops. Curious, restless, they tugged and rattled their chains. A louder growl came from the Alpha and silenced the others.

I faced him and established my authority.

"BAD DOG!" I shouted in a deep voice.

"BAD DOG!" I shook my fist at him.

STOMP! DOMINATE!

"BAD DOG!" He looked at me with hesitation.

The other dogs cowered as I threatened him. They knew what humans were.

Maintaining eye contact with the Alpha, "NO!"

STOMP!

I *must* be the Musher, *must* command their obedience but had no whip to
crack over their ears. I squared my shoulders, got BIG. My hands in fists, I raised my arms and swung them with authority.

STOMP! STOMP!

There was a narrow gap between dogs, and I had to weave my way through it.

Shouting: "OH, CA-NA-DA!"

I marched while stomping.

"OUR HOME AND NATIVE LAND!"

STOMP!

"TRUE PATRIOT LOVE IN ALL OUR SON'S COMMAND!"

STOMP! STOMP!

I looked them in the eyes.

"WITH GLOWING HEARTS, WE SEE THEE RISE,
THE TRUE NORTH STRONG AND FREE!"

STOMP!

"FROM FAR AND WIDE, OH CANADA,
WE STAND ON GUARD FOR THEE!"
"GOD KEEP OUR LAND GLORIOUS AND FREE!
OH CANADA, WE STAND ON GUARD FOR THEE!
OH CANADA, WE STAND ON GUARD FOR THEE!"

Once I'm beyond the pack, "STAY!", before I turned my back on them.

My heart was racing. The dogs were pacing.

I breathed deeply, thankfully before I attempted to locate the hotel. I did not know where I was, only that the Hotel was on the shore.

I stared up hoping that a Tern's white belly and black cap would glide by. There! The portent of my direction, I followed. Every step, a careful step – my eyes stole only a quick glance at my red boot laces.

I saw the shore and gained it. *Breathe deep.* I knew where to go and how to get there. The sea drew my map. Just beyond my red boot laces, a glimmer. I knelt in the sand, fingers brushing. Gold! A Gold chain with a locket. Inscribed on the locket: *Sara.*

She must have dropped it looking out to the sea. Chain and locket in hand, I looked seaward and back. Then, another anomaly - a metal post in the ground. On the post, Sara's postscript.

She came to Grise Fiord as a young teacher, wandered out on the Tundra and was killed by the sled dog pack. She was interred with that chain and locket round her neck. I was standing on her grave.

The Permafrost moves and heaves with every seasonal change.

This woman was an adventurer like me – her skin, once soft as an Arctic Willow Bud, her spirit, tenacious and precious as Arctic flowers that sleep in darkness for eleven months, burst into bloom for two short weeks and fade.

I knelt in communion, placed my hand where I imagined her heart to be and said a prayer – not to God but to the spirit that we shared. I dug a hole and buried the chain and locket there.

Sara taught me my Rite of the North-West Passage. As I walked back on the shore, my red boot laces transcended the tundra.

-Harris Taylor